ADRIFT IN NEW YORK

OR

TOM AND FLORENCE BRAVING THE WORLD

Horatio Alger, Jr.

Adrift in New York

Horatio Alger, Jr.

PO Box 2211
Fairfield, IA 52556
www.1stworldlibrary.com
First Edition

LCCN: 2006935234

Softcover ISBN: 1-4218-2487-6
Hardcover ISBN: 1-4218-2387-X
eBook ISBN: 1-4218-2587-2

1st World Library Literary Society

Giving Back to the World

"If you want to work on the core problem, it's early school literacy."

- James Barksdale, former CEO of Netscape

"No skill is more crucial to the future of a child, or to a democratic and prosperous society, than literacy."

- Los Angeles Times

Literacy... means far more than learning how to read and write... The aim is to transmit... knowledge and promote social participation."

- UNESCO

"Literacy is not a luxury, it is a right and a responsibility. If our world is to meet the challenges of the twenty-first century we must harness the energy and creativity of all our citizens."

- President Bill Clinton

"Parents should be encouraged to read to their children, and teachers should be equipped with all available techniques for teaching literacy, so the varying needs and capacities of individual kids can be taken into account."

- Hugh Mackay

CHAPTER I

THE MISSING HEIR

"Uncle, you are not looking well to-night."

"I'm not well, Florence. I sometimes doubt if I shall ever be any better."

"Surely, uncle, you cannot mean -"

"Yes, my child, I have reason to believe that I am nearing the end."

"I cannot bear to hear you speak so, uncle," said Florence Linden, in irrepressible agitation. "You are not an old man. You are but fifty-four."

"True, Florence, but it is not years only that make a man old. Two great sorrows have embittered my life. First, the death of my dearly beloved wife, and next, the loss of my boy, Harvey."

"It is long since I have heard you refer to my cousin's loss. I thought you had become reconciled - no, I do not mean that, - I thought your regret might be less poignant."

"I have not permitted myself to speak of it, but I have

never ceased to think of it day and night."

John Linden paused sadly, then resumed:

"If he had died, I might, as you say, have become reconciled; but he was abducted at the age of four by a revengeful servant whom I had discharged from my employment. Heaven knows whether he is living or dead, but it is impressed upon my mind that he still lives, it may be in misery, it may be as a criminal, while I, his unhappy father, live on in luxury which I cannot enjoy, with no one to care for me -"

Florence Linden sank impulsively on her knees beside her uncle's chair.

"Don't say that, uncle," she pleaded. "You know that I love you, Uncle John."

"And I, too, uncle."

There was a shade of jealousy in the voice of Curtis Waring as he entered the library through the open door, and approaching his uncle, pressed his hand.

He was a tall, dark-complexioned man, of perhaps thirty-five, with shifty, black eyes and thin lips, shaded by a dark mustache. It was not a face to trust.

Even when he smiled the expression of his face did not soften. Yet he could moderate his voice so as to express tenderness and sympathy.

He was the son of an elder sister of Mr. Linden, while Florence was the daughter of a younger brother.

Both were orphans, and both formed a part of Mr. Linden's household, and owed everything to his bounty.

Curtis was supposed to be in some business down-town; but he received a liberal allowance from his uncle, and often drew upon him for outside assistance.

As he stood with his uncle's hand in his, he was necessarily brought near Florence, who instinctively drew a little away, with a slight shudder indicating repugnance.

Slight as it was, Curtis detected it, and his face darkened.

John Linden looked from one to the other. "Yes," he said, "I must not forget that I have a nephew and a niece. You are both dear to me, but no one can take the place of the boy I have lost."

"But it is so long ago, uncle," said Curtis. "It must be fourteen years."

"It is fourteen years."

"And the boy is long since dead!"

"No, no!" said John Linden, vehemently. "I do not, I will not, believe it. He still lives, and I live only in the hope of one day clasping him in my arms."

"That is very improbable, uncle," said Curtis, in a tone of annoyance. "There isn't one chance in a hundred that my cousin still lives. The grave has closed over him long since. The sooner you make up your mind to accept the inevitable the better."

The drawn features of the old man showed that the words had a depressing effect upon his mind, but Florence interrupted her cousin with an indignant protest.

"How can you speak so, Curtis?" she exclaimed. "Leave Uncle John the hope that he has so long cherished. I have a presentiment that Harvey still lives."

John Linden's face brightened up

"You, too, believe it possible, Florence?" he said, eagerly.

"Yes, uncle. I not only believe it possible, but probable. How old would Harvey be if he still lived?"

"Eighteen - nearly a year older than yourself."

"How strange! I always think of him as a little boy."

"And I, too, Florence. He rises before me in his little velvet suit, as he was when I last saw him, with his sweet, boyish face, in which his mother's looks were reflected."

"Yet, if still living," interrupted Curtis, harshly, "he is a rough street boy, perchance serving his time at Blackwell's Island, and, a hardened young ruffian, whom it would be bitter mortification to recognize as your son."

"That's the sorrowful part of it," said his uncle, in a voice of anguish. "That is what I most dread."

"Then, since even if he were living you would not care

to recognize him, why not cease to think of him, or else regard him as dead?"

"Curtis Waring, have you no heart?" demanded Florence, indignantly.

"Indeed, Florence, you ought to know," said Curtis, sinking his voice into softly modulated accents.

"I know nothing of it," said Florence, coldly, rising from her recumbent position, and drawing aloof from Curtis.

"You know that the dearest wish of my heart is to find favor in your eyes. Uncle, you know my wish, and approve of it, do you not?"

"Yes, Curtis; you and Florence are equally dear to me, and it is my hope that you may be united. In that case, there will be no division of my fortune. It will be left to you jointly."

"Believe me, sir," said Curtis, with faltering voice, feigning an emotion which he did not feel, "believe me, that I fully appreciate your goodness. I am sure Florence joins with me -"

"Florence can speak for herself," said his cousin, coldly. "My uncle needs no assurance from me. He is always kind, and I am always grateful."

John Linden seemed absorbed in thought.

"I do not doubt your affection," he said; "and I have shown it by making you my joint heirs in the event of your marriage; but it is only fair to say that my property goes to my boy, if he still lives."

"But, sir," protested Curtis, "is not that likely to create unnecessary trouble? It can never be known, and meanwhile -"

"You and Florence will hold the property in trust."

"Have you so specified in your will?" asked Curtis.

"I have made two wills. Both are in yonder secretary. By the first the property is bequeathed to you and Florence. By the second and later, it goes to my lost boy in the event of his recovery. Of course, you and Florence are not forgotten, but the bulk of the property goes to Harvey."

"I sincerely wish the boy might be restored to you," said Curtis; but his tone belied his words. "Believe me, the loss of the property would affect me little, if you could be made happy by realizing your warmest desire; but, uncle, I think it only the part of a friend to point out to you, as I have already done, the baselessness of any such expectation."

"It may be as you say, Curtis," said his uncle, with a sigh. "If I were thoroughly convinced of it, I would destroy the later will, and leave my property absolutely to you and Florence."

"No, uncle," said Florence, impulsively, "make no change; let the will stand."

Curtis, screened from his uncle's view, darted a glance of bitter indignation at Florence.

"Is the girl mad?" he muttered to himself. "Must she forever balk me?"

"Let it be so for the present, then," said Mr. Linden, wearily. "Curtis, will you ring the bell? I am tired, and shall retire to my couch early."

"Let me help you, Uncle John," said Florence, eagerly.

"It is too much for your strength, my child. I am growing more and more helpless."

"I, too, can help," said Curtis.

John Linden, supported on either side by his nephew and niece, left the room, and was assisted to his chamber.

Curtis and Florence returned to the library.

"Florence," said her cousin, "my uncle's intentions, as expressed to-night, make it desirable that there should be an understanding between us. Take a seat beside me" - leading her to a sofa - "and let us talk this matter over."

With a gesture of repulsion Florence declined the proffered seat, and remained standing.

"As you please," she answered, coldly.

"Will you be seated?"

"No; our interview will be brief."

"Then I will come to the point. Uncle John wishes to

see us united."

"It can never be!" said Florence, decidedly.

Curtis bit his lip in mortification, for her tone was cold and scornful.

Mingled with this mortification was genuine regret, for, so far as he was capable of loving any one, he loved his fair young cousin.

"You profess to love Uncle John, and yet you would disappoint his cherished hope!" he returned.

"Is it his cherished hope?"

"There is no doubt about it. He has spoken to me more than once on the subject. Feeling that his end is near, he wishes to leave you in charge of a protector."

"I can protect myself," said Florence, proudly.

"You think so. You do not consider the hapless lot of a penniless girl in a cold and selfish world."

"Penniless?" repeated Florence, in an accent of surprise.

"Yes, penniless. Our uncle's bequest to you is conditional upon your acceptance of my hand."

"Has he said this?" asked Florence, sinking into an armchair, with a helpless look.

"He has told me so more than once," returned Curtis, smoothly. "You don't know how near to his heart this marriage is. I know what you would say: If the property comes to me I could come to your assistance, but I am expressly prohibited from doing so. I have pleaded with my uncle in your behalf, but in vain."

Florence was too clear-sighted not to penetrate his falsehood.

"If my uncle's heart is hardened against me," she said, "I shall be too wise to turn to you. I am to understand, then, that my choice lies between poverty and a union with you?"

"You have stated it correctly, Florence."

"Then," said Florence, arising, "I will not hesitate. I shrink from poverty, for I have been reared in luxury, but I will sooner live in a hovel -"

"Or a tenement house," interjected Curtis, with a sneer.

"Yes, or a tenement house, than become the wife of one I loathe."

"Girl, you shall bitterly repent that word!" said Curtis, stung to fury.

She did not reply, but, pale and sorrowful, glided from the room to weep bitter tears in the seclusion of her chamber.

CHAPTER II

A STRANGER VISITOR

Curtis Waring followed the retreating form of his cousin with a sardonic smile.

"She is in the toils! She cannot escape me!" he muttered. "But" - and here his brow darkened - "it vexes me to see how she repels my advances, as if I were some loathsome thing! If only she would return my love - for I do love her, cold as she is - I should be happy. Can there be a rival? But no! we live so quietly that she has met no one who could win her affection. Why can she not turn to me? Surely, I am not so ill-favored, and though twice her age, I am still a young man. Nay, it is only a young girl's caprice. She shall yet come to my arms, a willing captive."

His thoughts took a turn, as he arose from his seat, and walked over to the secretary.

"So it is here that the two wills are deposited!" he said to himself; "one making me a rich man, the other a beggar! While the last is in existence I am not safe. The boy may be alive, and liable to turn up at any moment. If only he were dead - or the will destroyed -" Here he made a suggestive pause.

He took a bunch of keys from his pocket, and tried one after another, but without success. He was so absorbed in his work that he did not notice the entrance of a dark-browed, broad-shouldered man, dressed in a shabby corduroy suit, till the intruder indulged in a short cough, intended to draw attention.

Starting with guilty consciousness, Curtis turned sharply around, and his glance fell on the intruder.

"Who are you?" he demanded, angrily. "And how dare you enter a gentleman's house unbidden?"

"Are you the gentleman?" asked the intruder, with intentional insolence.

"Yes."

"You own this house?"

"Not at present. It is my uncle's."

"And that secretary - pardon my curiosity - is his?"

"Yes; but what business is it of yours?"

"Not much. Only it makes me laugh to see a gentleman picking a lock. You should leave such business to men like me!"

"You are an insolent fellow!" said Curtis, more embarrassed than he liked to confess, for this rough-looking man had become possessed of a dangerous secret. "I am my uncle's confidential agent, and it was on business of his that I wished to open the desk."

"Why not go to him for the key?"

"Because he is sick. But, pshaw! why should I apologize or give any explanation to you? What can you know of him or me?"

"More, perhaps, than you suspect," said the intruder, quietly.

"Then, you know, perhaps, that I am my uncle's heir?"

"Don't be too sure of that."

"Look here, fellow," said Curtis, thoroughly provoked, "I don't know who you are nor what you mean, but let me inform you that your presence here is an intrusion, and the sooner you leave the house the better!"

"I will leave it when I get ready."

Curtis started to his feet, and advanced to his visitor with an air of menace.

"Go at once," he exclaimed, angrily, "or I will kick you out of the door!"

"What's the matter with the window?" returned the stranger, with an insolent leer.

"That's as you prefer, but if you don't leave at once I will eject you."

By way of reply, the rough visitor coolly seated himself in a luxurious easy-chair, and, looking up into the angry face of Waring, said:

"Oh, no, you won't."

"And why not, may I ask?" said Curtis, with a feeling of uneasiness for which he could not account.

"Why not? Because, in that case, I should seek an interview with your uncle, and tell him -"

"What?"

"That his son still lives; and that I can restore him to his -"

The face of Curtis Waring blanched; he staggered as if he had been struck; and he cried out, hoarsely:

"It is a lie!"

"It is the truth, begging your pardon. Do you mind my smoking?" and he coolly produced a common clay pipe, filled and lighted it.

"Who are you?" asked Curtis, scanning the man's features with painful anxiety.

"Have you forgotten Tim Bolton?"

"Are you Tim Bolton?" faltered Curtis.

"Yes; but you don't seem glad to see me?"

"I thought you were -"

"In Australia. So I was three years since. Then I got homesick, and came back to New York."

"You have been here three years?"

"Yes," chuckled Bolton. "You didn't suspect it, did you?"

"Where?" asked Curtis, in a hollow voice.

"I keep a saloon on the Bowery. There's my card. Call around when convenient."

Curtis was about to throw the card into the grate, but on second thought dropped it into his pocket.

"And the boy?" he asked, slowly.

"Is alive and well. He hasn't been starved. Though I dare say you wouldn't have grieved if he had."

"And he is actually in this city?"

"Just so."

"Does he know anything of - you know what I mean."

"He doesn't know that he is the son of a rich man, and heir to the property which you look upon as yours. That's what you mean, isn't it?"

"Yes. What is he doing? Is he at work?"

"He helps me some in the saloon, sells papers in the evenings, and makes himself generally useful."

"Has he any education?"

"Well, I haven't sent him to boarding school or

college," answered Tim. "He don't know no Greek, or Latin, or mathematics - phew, that's a hard word. You didn't tell me you wanted him made a scholar of."

"I didn't. I wanted never to see or hear from him again. What made you bring him back to New York?"

"Couldn't keep away, governor. I got homesick, I did. There ain't but one Bowery in the world, and I hankered after that -"

"Didn't I pay you money to keep away, Tim Bolton?"

"I don't deny it; but what's three thousand dollars? Why, the kid's cost me more than that. I've had the care of him for fourteen years, and it's only about two hundred a year."

"You have broken your promise to me!" said Curtis, sternly.

"There's worse things than breaking your promise," retorted Bolton.

Scarcely had he spoken than a change came over his face, and he stared open-mouthed behind him and beyond Curtis.

Startled himself, Curtis turned, and saw, with a feeling akin to dismay, the tall figure of his uncle standing on the threshold of the left portal, clad in a morning gown, with his eyes fixed inquiringly upon Bolton and himself.

CHAPTER III

AN UNHOLY COMPACT

"Who is that man, Curtis?" asked John Linden, pointing his thin finger at Tim Bolton, who looked strangely out of place, as, with clay pipe, he sat in the luxurious library on a sumptuous chair.

"That man?" stammered Curtis, quite at a loss what to say.

"Yes."

"He is a poor man out of luck, who has applied to me for assistance," answered Curtis, recovering his wits.

"That's it, governor," said Bolton, thinking it necessary to confirm the statement. "I've got five small children at home almost starvin', your honor."

"That is sad. What is your business, my man?"

It was Bolton's turn to be embarrassed.

"My business?" he repeated.

"That is what I said."

"I'm a blacksmith, but I'm willing to do any honest work."

"That is commendable; but don't you know that it is very ill-bred to smoke a pipe in a gentleman's house?"

"Excuse me, governor!"

And Bolton extinguished his pipe, and put it away in a pocket of his corduroy coat.

"I was just telling him the same thing," said Curtis. "Don't trouble yourself any further, uncle. I will inquire into the man's circumstances, and help him if I can."

"Very well, Curtis. I came down because I thought I heard voices."

John Linden slowly returned to his chamber, and left the two alone.

"The governor's getting old," said Bolton. "When I was butler here, fifteen years ago, he looked like a young man. He didn't suspect that he had ever seen me before."

"Nor that you had carried away his son, Bolton."

"Who hired me to do it? Who put me up to the job, as far as that goes?"

"Hush! Walls have ears. Let us return to business."

"That suits me."

"Look here, Tim Bolton," said Curtis, drawing up a chair, and lowering his voice to a confidential pitch, "you say you want money?"

"Of course I do."

"Well, I don't give money for nothing."

"I know that. What's wanted now?"

"You say the boy is alive?"

"He's very much alive."

"Is there any necessity for his living?" asked Curtis, in a sharp, hissing tone, fixing his eyes searchingly on Bolton, to see how his hint would be taken.

"You mean that you want me to murder him?" said Bolton, quickly.

"Why not? You don't look over scrupulous."

"I am a bad man, I admit it," said Bolton, with a gesture of repugnance, "a thief, a low blackguard, perhaps, but, thank Heaven! I am no murderer! And if I was, I wouldn't spill a drop of that boy's blood for the fortune that is his by right."

"I didn't give you credit for so much sentiment, Bolton," said Curtis, with a sneer. "You don't look like it, but appearances are deceitful. We'll drop the subject. You can serve me in another way. Can you open this secretary?"

"Yes; that's in my line."

"There is a paper in it that I want. It is my uncle's will. I have a curiosity to read it."

"I understand. Well, I'm agreeable."

"If you find any money or valuables, you are welcome to them. I only want the paper. When will you make the attempt?"

"To-morrow night. When will it be safe?"

"At eleven o'clock. We all retire early in this house. Can you force an entrance?"

"Yes; but it will be better for you to leave the outer door unlocked."

"I have a better plan. Here is my latchkey."

"Good! I may not do the job myself, but I will see that it is done. How shall I know the will?"

"It is in a big envelope, tied with a narrow tape. Probably it is inscribed: 'My will.'"

"Suppose I succeed, when shall I see you?"

"I will come around to your place on the Bowery. Good-night!"

Curtis Waring saw Bolton to the door, and let him out. Returning, he flung himself on a sofa.

"I can make that man useful!" he reflected. "There is an element of danger in the boy's presence in New York; but it will go hard if I can't get rid of him! Tim

Bolton is unexpectedly squeamish, but there are others to whom I can apply. With gold everything is possible. It's time matters came to a finish. My uncle's health is rapidly failing - the doctor hints that he has heart disease - and the fortune for which I have been waiting so long will soon be mine, if I work my cards right. I can't afford to make any mistakes now."

CHAPTER IV

FLORENCE

Florence Linden sat in the library the following evening in an attitude of depression. Her eyelids were swollen, and it was evident she had been weeping. During the day she had had an interview with her uncle, in which he harshly insisted upon her yielding to his wishes, and marrying her cousin, Curtis.

"But, uncle," she objected, "I do not love him."

"Marry him, and love will come."

"Never!" she said, vehemently.

"You speak confidently, miss," said Mr. Linden, with irritation.

"Listen, Uncle John. It is not alone that I do not love him. I dislike him - I loathe - him."

"Nonsense! that is a young girl's extravagant nonsense."

"No, uncle."

"There can be no reason for such a foolish dislike.

What can you have against him?"

"It is impressed upon me, uncle, that Curtis is a bad man. There is something false - treacherous - about him."

"Pooh! child! you are more foolish than I thought. I don't say Curtis is an angel. No man is; at least, I never met any such. But he is no worse than the generality of men. In marrying him you will carry out my cherished wish. Florence, I have not long to live. I shall be glad to see you well established in life before I leave you. As the wife of Curtis you will have a recognized position. You will go on living in this house, and the old home will be maintained."

"But why is it necessary for me to marry at all, Uncle John?"

"You will be sure to marry some one. Should I divide my fortune between you and Curtis, you would become the prey of some unscrupulous fortune hunter."

"Better that than become the wife of Curtis Waring -"

"I see, you are incorrigible," said her uncle, angrily. "Do you refuse obedience to my wishes?"

"Command me in anything else, Uncle John, and I will obey," pleaded Florence.

"Indeed! You only thwart me in my cherished wish, but are willing to obey me in unimportant matters. You forget the debt you owe me."

"I forget nothing, dear uncle. I do not forget that, when

I was a poor little child, helpless and destitute, you took me in your arms, gave me a home, and have cared for me from that time to this as only a parent could."

"You remember that, then?"

"Yes, uncle. I hope you will not consider me wholly ungrateful."

"It only makes matters worse. You own your obligations, yet refuse to make the only return I desire. You refuse to comfort me in the closing days of my life by marrying your cousin."

"Because that so nearly concerns my happiness that no one has a right to ask me to sacrifice all I hold dear."

"I see you are incorrigible," said John Linden, stormily. "Do you know what will be the consequences?"

"I am prepared for all."

"Then listen! If you persist in balking me, I shall leave the entire estate to Curtis."

"Do with your money as you will, uncle. I have no claim to more than I have received."

"You are right there; but that is not all."

Florence fixed upon him a mute look of inquiry.

"I will give you twenty-four hours more to come to your senses. Then, if you persist in your ingratitude and disobedience, you must find another home."

"Oh, uncle, you do not mean that?" exclaimed Florence, deeply moved.

"I do mean it, and I shall not allow your tears to move me. Not another word, for I will not hear it. Take twenty-four hours to think over what I have said."

Florence bowed her head on her hands, and gave herself up to sorrowful thoughts. But she was interrupted by the entrance of the servant, who announced:

"Mr. Percy de Brabazon."

An effeminate-looking young man, foppishly dressed, followed the servant into the room, and made it impossible for Florence to deny herself, as she wished to do.

"I hope I see you well, Miss Florence," he simpered.

"Thank you, Mr. de Brabazon," said Florence, coldly. "I have a slight headache."

"I am awfully sorry, I am, upon my word, Miss Florence. My doctor tells me it is only those whose bwains are vewy active that are troubled with headaches."

"Then, I presume, Mr. de Brabazon," said Florence, with intentional sarcasm, "that you never have a headache."

"Weally, Miss Florence, that is vewy clevah. You will have your joke."

"It was no joke, I assure you, Mr. de Brabazon."

"I - I thought it might be. Didn't I see you at the opewa last evening?"

"Possibly. I was there."

"I often go to the opewa. It's so - so fashionable, don't you know?"

"Then you don't go to hear the music?"

"Oh, of course, but one can't always be listening to the music, don't you know. I had a fwiend with me last evening - an Englishman - a charming fellow, I assure you. He's the second cousin of a lord, and yet - you'll hardly credit it - we're weally vewy intimate. He tells me, Miss Florence, that I'm the perfect image of his cousin, Lord Fitz Noodle."

"I am not at all surprised."

"Weally, you are vewy kind, Miss Florence. I thought it a great compliment. I don't know how it is, but evewybody takes me for an Englishman. Strange, isn't it?"

"I am very glad."

"May I ask why, Miss Florence?"

"Because - Well, perhaps I had better not explain. It seems to give you pleasure. You would, probably, prefer to be an Englishman."

"I admit that I have a great admiration for the English character. It's a gweat pity we have no lords in America. Now, if you would only allow me to bring my English fwiend here -

"I don't care to make any new acquaintances. Even if I did, I prefer my own countrymen. Don't you like America, Mr. de Brabazon?"

"Oh, of courth, if we only had some lords here."

"We have plenty of flunkeys."

"That's awfully clevah, 'pon my word."

"Is it? I am afraid you are too complimentary. You are very good-natured."

"I always feel good-natured in your company, Miss Florence. I - wish I could always be with you."

"Really! Wouldn't that be a trifle monotonous?" asked Florence, sarcastically.

"Not if we were married," said Percy, boldly breaking the ice.

"What do you mean, Mr. de Brabazon?"

"I hope you will excuse me, Miss Florence - Miss Linden, I mean; but I'm awfully in love with you, and have been ever so long - but I never dared to tell you so. I felt so nervous, don't you know? Will you marry me? I'll be awfully obliged if you will."

Mr. de Brabazon rather awkwardly slipped from his chair, and sank on one knee before Florence.

"Please arise, Mr. de Brabazon," said Florence,

hurriedly. "It is quite out of the question - what you ask - I assure you."

"Ah! I see how it is," said Percy, clasping his hands sadly. "You love another."

"Not that I am aware of."

"Then I may still hope?"

"I cannot encourage you, Mr. de Brabazon. My heart is free, but it can never be yours."

"Then," said Percy, gloomily, "there is only one thing for me to do."

"What is that?"

"I shall go to the Bwooklyn Bwidge, climb to the parapet, jump into the water, and end my misewable life."

"You had better think twice before adopting such a desperate resolution, Mr. de Brabazon. You will meet others who will be kinder to you than I have been -"

"I can never love another. My heart is broken. Farewell, cruel girl. When you read the papers tomorrow morning, think of the unhappy Percy de Brabazon!"

Mr. de Brabazon folded his arms gloomily, and stalked out of the room.

"If my position were not so sad, I should be tempted to smile," said Florence. "Mr. de Brabazon will not do this thing. His emotions are as strong as those of a butterfly."

After a brief pause Florence seated herself at the table, and drew toward her writing materials.

"It is I whose heart should be broken!" she murmured; "I who am driven from the only home I have ever known. What can have turned against me my uncle, usually so kind and considerate? It must be that Curtis has exerted a baneful influence upon him. I cannot leave him without one word of farewell."

She took up a sheet of paper, and wrote, rapidly:

> "Dear Uncle: You have told me to leave your house, and I obey. I cannot tell you how sad I feel, when I reflect that I have lost your love, and must go forth among strangers - I know not where. I was but a little girl when you gave me a home. I have grown up in an atmosphere of love, and I have felt very grateful to you for all you have done for me. I have tried to conform to your wishes, and I would obey you in all else - but I cannot marry Curtis; I think I would rather die. Let me still live with you as I have done. I do not care for any part of your money - leave it all to him, if you think best - but give me back my place in your heart. You are angry now, but you will some time pity and forgive your poor Florence, who will never cease to bless and pray for you. Good-bye!
>
> "Florence."

She was about to sign herself Florence Linden, but reflected that she was no longer entitled to use a name which would seem to carry with it a claim upon her uncle.

The tears fell upon the paper as she was writing, but she heeded them not. It was the saddest hour of her life. Hitherto she had been shielded from all sorrow, and secure in the affection of her uncle, had never dreamed that there would come a time when she would feel obliged to leave all behind her, and go out into the world, friendless and penniless, but poorest of all in the loss of that love which she had hitherto enjoyed.

After completing the note, Florence let her head fall upon the table, and sobbed herself to sleep.

An hour and a half passed, the servant looked in, but noticing that her mistress was sleeping, contented herself with lowering the gas, but refrained from waking her.

And so she slept on till the French clock upon the mantle struck eleven.

Five minutes later and the door of the room slowly opened, and a boy entered on tiptoe. He was roughly dressed. His figure was manly and vigorous, and despite his stealthy step and suspicious movements his face was prepossessing.

He started when he saw Florence.

"What, a sleeping gal!" he said to himself. "Tim told me I'd find the coast clear, but I guess she's sound asleep, and won't hear nothing. I don't half like this job, but I've got to do as Tim told me. He says he's my father, so I s'pose it's all right. All the same, I shall be nabbed some day, and then the family'll be disgraced.

It's a queer life I've led ever since I can remember. Sometimes I feel like leaving Tim, and settin' up for myself. I wonder how 'twould seem to be respectable."

The boy approached the secretary, and with some tools he had brought essayed to open it. After a brief delay he succeeded, and lifted the cover. He was about to explore it, according to Tim's directions, when he heard a cry of fear, and turning swiftly saw Florence, her eyes dilated with terror, gazing at him.

"Who are you?" she asked in alarm, "and what are you doing there?"

CHAPTER V

DODGER

The boy sprang to the side of Florence, and siezed her wrists in his strong young grasp.

"Don't you alarm the house," he said, "or I'll -"

"What will you do?" gasped Florence, in alarm. The boy was evidently softened by her beauty, and answered in a tone of hesitation:

"I don't know. I won't harm you if you keep quiet."

"What are you here for?" asked Florence, fixing her eyes on the boy's face; "are you a thief?"

"I don't know - yes, I suppose I am."

"How sad, when you are so young."

"What! miss, do you pity me?"

"Yes, my poor boy, you must be very poor, or you wouldn't bring yourself to steal."

"No. I ain't poor; leastways, I have enough to eat, and I have a place to sleep."

"Then why don't you earn your living by honest means?"

"I can't; I must obey orders."

"Whose orders?"

"Why, the guv'nor's, to be sure."

"Did he tell you to open that secretary?"

"Yes."

"Who is the guv'nor, as you call him?"

"I can't tell; it wouldn't be square."

"He must be a very wicked man."

"Well, he ain't exactly what you call an angel, but I've seen wuss men than the guv'nor."

"Do you mind telling me your own name?"

"No; for I know you won't peach on me. Tom Dodger."

"Dodger?"

"Yes."

"That isn't a surname."

"It's all I've got. That's what I'm always called."

"It is very singular," said Florence, fixing a glance of mingled curiosity and perplexity upon the young visitor.

While the two were earnestly conversing in that subdued light, afforded by the lowered gaslight, Tim Bolton crept in through the door unobserved by either, tiptoed across the room to the secretary, snatched the will and a roll of bills, and escaped without attracting attention.

"Oh, I wish I could persuade you to give up this bad life," resumed Florence, earnestly, "and become honest."

"Do you really care what becomes of me, miss?" asked Dodger, slowly.

"I do, indeed."

"That's very kind of you, miss; but I don't understand it. You are a rich young lady, and I'm only a poor boy, livin' in a Bowery dive."

"What's that?"

"Never mind, miss, such as you wouldn't understand. Why, all my life I've lived with thieves, and drunkards, and bunco men, and -"

"But I'm sure you don't like it. You are fit for something better."

"Do you really think so?" asked Dodger, doubtfullly.

"Yes; you have a good face. You were meant to be good and honest, I am sure."

"Would you trust me?" asked the boy, earnestly, fixing his large, dark eyes eloquently on the face of Florence.

"Yes, I would if you would only leave your evil companions, and become true to your better nature."

"No one ever spoke to me like that before, miss," said Dodger, his expressive features showing that he was strongly moved. "You think I could be good if I tried hard, and grow up respectable?"

"I am sure you could," said Florence, confidently.

There was something in this boy, young outlaw though he was, that moved her powerfully, and even fascinated her, though she hardly realized it. It was something more than a feeling of compassion for a wayward and misguided youth.

"I could if I was rich like you, and lived in a nice house, and 'sociated with swells. If you had a father like mine -"

"Is he a bad man?"

"Well, he don't belong to the church. He keeps a gin mill, and has ever since I was a kid."

"Have you always lived with him?"

"Yes, but not in New York."

"Where then?"

"In Melbourne."

"That's in Australia."

"Yes, miss."

"How long since you came to New York?"

"I guess it's about three years."

"And you have always had this man as a guardian? Poor boy!"

"You've got a different father from me, miss?"

Tears forced themselves to the eyes of Florence, as this remark brought forcibly to her mind the position in which she was placed.

"Alas!" she answered, impulsively, "I am alone in the world!"

"What! ain't the old gentleman that lives here your father?"

"He is my uncle; but he is very, very angry with me, and has this very day ordered me to leave the house."

"Why, what a cantankerous old ruffian he is, to be sure!" exclaimed the boy, indignantly.

"Hush! you must not talk against my uncle. He has always been kind to me till now."

"Why, what's up? What's the old gentleman mad about?"

"He wants me to marry my cousin Curtis - a man I do not even like."

"That's a shame! Is it the dude I saw come out of the house a little while ago?"

"Oh, no; that's a different gentleman. It's Mr. de Brabazon."

"You don't want to marry him, do you?"

"No, no!"

"I'm glad of that. He don't look as if he knew enough to come in when it rained."

"The poor young man is not very brilliant, but I think I would rather marry him than Curtis Waring."

"I've seen him, too. He's got dark hair and a dark complexion, and a wicked look in his eye."

"You, too, have noticed that?"

"I've seen such as him before. He's a bad man."

"Do you know anything about him?" asked Florence, eagerly.

"Only his looks."

"I am not deceived," murmured Florence, "it's not wholly prejudice. The boy distrusts him, too. So you see, Dodger," she added, aloud, "I am not a rich young lady, as you suppose. I must leave this house, and work for my living. I have no home any more."

"If you have no home," said Dodger, impulsively, "come home with me."

"To the home you have described, my poor boy? How could I do that?"

"No; I will hire a room for you in a quiet street, and you shall be my sister. I will work for you, and give you my money."

"You are kind, and I am glad to think I have found a friend when I need one most. But I could not accept stolen money. It would be as bad as if I, too, were a thief."

"I am not a thief! That is, I won't be any more."

"And you will give up your plan of robbing my uncle?"

"Yes, I will; though I don't know what my guv'nor will say. He'll half murder me, I expect. He'll be sure to cut up rough."

"Do right, Dodger, whatever happens. Promise me that you will never steal again?"

"There's my hand, miss - I promise. Nobody ever talked to me like you. I never thought much about bein' respectable, and growin' up to be somebody, but if you takc an interest in me, I'll try hard to do right."

At this moment, Mr. Linden, clad in a long morning gown, and holding a candle in his hand, entered the room, and started in astonishment when he saw Florence clasping the hand of one whose appearance led him to stamp as a young rough.

"Shameless girl!" he exclaimed, in stern reproof. "So this is the company you keep when you think I am out of the way!"

CHAPTER VI

A TEMPEST

The charge was so strange and unexpected that Florence was overwhelmed. She could only murmur:

"Oh, uncle!"

Her young companion was indignant. Already he felt that Florence had consented to accept him as a friend, and he was resolved to stand by her.

"I say, old man," he bristled up, "don't you go to insult her! She's an angel!"

"No doubt you think so," rejoined Mr. Linden, in a tone of sarcasm. "Upon my word, miss, I congratulate you on your elevated taste. So this is your reason for not being willing to marry your Cousin Curtis?"

"Indeed, uncle, you are mistaken. I never met this boy till to-night."

"Don't try to deceive me. Young man, did you open my secretary?"

"Yes, sir."

"And robbed it into the bargain," continued Linden, going to the secretary, and examining it. He did not, however, miss the will, but only the roll of bills. "Give me back the money you have taken from me, you young rascal!"

"I took nothing, sir."

"It's a lie! The money is gone, and no one else could have taken it."

"I don't allow no one to call me a liar. Just take that back, old man, or I -"

"Indeed, uncle, he took nothing, for he had only just opened the secretary when I woke up and spoke to him."

"You stand by him, of course, shameless girl! I blush to think that you are my niece. I am glad to think that my eyes are opened before it is too late."

The old merchant rang the bell violently, and aroused the house. Dodger made no attempt to escape, but stood beside Florence in the attitude of a protector. But a short time elapsed before Curtis Waring and the servants entered the room, and gazed with wonder at the *tableau* presented by the excited old man and the two young people.

"My friends," said John Linden, in a tone of excitement, "I call you to witness that this girl, whom I blush to acknowledge as my niece, has proved herself unworthy of my kindness. In your presence I cut her off, and bid her never again darken my door."

"But what has she done, uncle?" asked Curtis. He was prepared for the presence of Dodger, whom he rightly concluded to be the agent of Tim Bolton, but he could not understand why Florence should be in the library at this late hour. Nor was he able to understand the evidently friendly relations between her and the young visitor.

"What has she done?" repeated John Linden. "She has introduced that young ruffian into the house to rob me. Look at that secretary! He has forced it open, and stolen a large sum of money."

"It is not true, sir," said Dodger, calmly, "about taking the money, I mean. I haven't taken a cent."

"Then why did you open the secretary?"

"I did mean to take money, but she stopped me."

"Oh, she stopped you?" repeated Linden, with withring sarcasm. "Then, perhaps, you will tell me where the money is gone?"

"He hasn't discovered about the will," thought Curtis, congratulating himself; "if the boy has it, I must manage to give him a chance to escape."

"You can search me if you want to," continued Dodger, proudly. "You won't find no money on me."

"Do you think I am a fool, you young burglar?" exclaimed John Linden, angrily.

"Uncle, let me speak to the boy," said Curtis, soothingly. "I think he will tell me."

"As you like, Curtis; but I am convinced that he is a thief."

Curtis Waring beckoned Dodger into an adjoining room.

"Now, my boy," he said, smoothly, "give me what you took from the secretary, and I will see that you are not arrested."

"But, sir, I didn't take nothing - it's just as I told the old duffer. The girl waked up just as I'd got the secretary open, and I didn't have a chance."

"But the money is gone," said Curtis, in an incredulous tone.

"I don't know nothing about that."

"Come, you'd better examine your pockets. In the hurry of the moment you may have taken it without knowing it."

"No, I couldn't."

"Didn't you take a paper of any kind?" asked Curtis, eagerly. "Sometimes papers are of more value than money."

"No, I didn't take no paper, though Tim told me to."

Curtis quietly ignored the allusion to Tim, for it did not suit his purpose to get Tim into trouble. His unscrupulous agent knew too much that would compromise his principal.

"Are you willing that I should examine you?"

"Yes, I am. Go ahead."

Curtis thrust his hand into the pockets of the boy, who, boy as he was, was as tall as himself, but was not repaid by the discovery of anything. He was very much perplexed.

"Didn't you throw the articles on the floor?" he demanded, suspiciously.

"No, I didn't."

"You didn't give them to the young lady?"

"No; if I had she'd have said so."

"Humph! this is strange. What is your name?"

"Dodger."

"That's a queer name; have you no other?"

"Not as I know of."

"With whom do you live?"

"With my father. Leastways, he says he's my father."

There was a growing suspicion in the mind of Curtis Waring. He scanned the boy's features with attention. Could this ill-dressed boy - a street boy in appearance - be his long-lost and deeply wronged cousin?

"Who is it that says he is your father?" he demanded, abruptly.

"Do you want to get him into trouble?"

"No, I don't want to get him into trouble, or you either. Better tell me all, and I will be your friend."

"You're a better sort than I thought at first," said Dodger. "The man I live with is called Tim Bolton."

"I though so," quickly ejaculated Curtis. He had scarcely got out the words before he was sensible that he had made a mistake.

"What! do you know Tim?" inquired Dodger, in surprise.

"I mean," replied Curtis, lamely, "that I have heard of this man Bolton. He keeps a saloon on the Bowery, doesn't he?"

"Yes."

"I thought you would be living with some such man. Did he come to the house with you tonight?"

"Yes."

"Where is he?"

"He stayed outside."

"Perhaps he is there now."

"Don't you go to having him arrested," said Dodger, suspiciously.

"I will keep my promise. Are you sure you didn't pass

out the paper and the money to him? Think now."

"No, I didn't. I didn't have a chance. When I came into the room yonder I saw the gal asleep, and I thought she wouldn't hear me, but when I got the desk open she spoke to me, and asked me what I was doin'."

"And you took nothing?"

"No."

"It seems very strange. I cannot understand it. Yet my uncle says the money is gone. Did anyone else enter the room while you were talking with Miss Linden?"

"I didn't see any one."

"What were you talking about?"

"She said the old man wanted her to marry you, and she didn't want to."

"She told you that?" exclaimed Curtis, in displeasure.

"Yes, she did. She said she'd rather marry the dude that was here early this evenin'."

"Mr. de Brabazon!"

"Yes, that's the name."

"Upon my word, she was very confidential. You are a queer person for her to select as a confidant."

"Maybe so, sir; but she knows I'm her friend."

"You like the young lady, then? Perhaps you would like to marry her yourself?"

"As if she'd take any notice of a poor boy like me. I told her if her uncle sent her away, I'd take care of her and be a brother to her."

"How would Mr. Tim Bolton - that's his name, isn't it? - like that?"

"I wouldn't take her to where he lives."

"I think, myself, it would hardly be a suitable home for a young lady brought up on Madison Avenue. There is certainly no accounting for tastes. Miss Florence -"

"That's her name, is it?"

"Yes; didn't she tell you?"

"No; but it's a nice name."

"She declines my hand, and accepts your protection. It will certainly be a proud distinction to become Mrs. Dodger."

"Don't laugh at her!" said Dodger, suspiciously.

"I don't propose to. But I think we may as well return to the library."

"Well," said Mr. Linden, as his nephew returned with Dodger.

"I have examined the boy, and found nothing on his person," said Curtis; "I confess I am puzzled. He appears to have a high admiration for Florence -"

"As I supposed."

"She has even confided to him her dislike for me, and he has offered
her his protection."

"Is this so, miss?" demanded Mr. Linden, sternly.

"Yes, uncle," faltered Florence.

"Then you can join the young person you have selected whenever you please. For your sake I will not have him arrested for attempted burglary. He is welcome to what he has taken, since he is likely to marry into the family. You may stay here to-night, and he can call for you in the morning."

John Linden closed the secretary, and left the room, leaving Florence sobbing. The servants, too, retired, and Curtis was left alone with her.

"Florence," he said, "accept my hand, and I will reconcile my uncle to you. Say but the word, and -"

"I can never speak it, Curtis! I will take my uncle at his word. Dodger, call for me to-morrow at eight, and I will accept your friendly services in finding me a new home."

"I'll be on hand, miss. Good-night!"

"Be it so, obstinate girl!" said Curtis, angrily. "The time will come when you will bitterly repent your mad decision."

CHAPTER VII

FLORENCE LEAVES HOME

Florence passed a sleepless night. It had come upon her so suddenly, this expulsion from the home of her childhood, that she could not fully realize it. She could not feel that she was taking her last look at the familiar room, and well-remembered dining-room, where she had sat down for the last time for breakfast. She was alone at the breakfast table, for the usual hour was half-past eight, and she had appointed Dodger to call for her at eight.

"Is it true, Miss Florence, that you're going away?" asked Jane, the warm-hearted table girl, as she waited upon Florence.

"Yes, Jane," answered Florence, sadly.

"It's a shame, so it is! I didn't think your uncle would be so hard-hearted."

"He is disappointed because I won't marry my Cousin Curtis."

"I don't blame you for it, miss. I never liked Mr. Waring. He isn't half good enough for you."

"I say nothing about that, Jane; but I will not marry a man I do not love."

"Nor would I, miss. Where are you going, if I may make so bold?"

"I don't know, Jane," said Florence, despondently.

"But you can't walk about the streets."

"A trusty friend is going to call for me at eight o'clock; when he comes admit him."

"It is a - a young gentleman?"

"You wouldn't call him such. He is a boy, a poor boy; but I think he is a true friend. He says he will find me a comfortable room somewhere, where I can settle down and look for work."

"Are you going to work for a living, Miss Florence?" asked Jane, horrified.

"I must, Jane."

"It's a great shame - you, a lady born."

"No, Jane, I do not look upon it in that light. I shall be happier for having my mind and my hands occupied."

"What work will you do?"

"I don't know yet. Dodger will advise me."

"Who, miss?"

"Dodger."

"Who is he?"

"It's the boy I spoke of."

"Shure, he's got a quare name."

"Yes; but names don't count for much. It's the heart I think of, and this boy has a kind heart."

"Have you known him long?"

"I saw him yesterday for the first time."

"Is it the young fellow who was here last night?"

"Yes."

"He isn't fit company for the likes of you, Miss Florence."

"You forget, Jane, that I am no longer a rich young lady. I am poorer than even you. This Dodger is kind, and I feel that I can trust him."

"If you are poor, Miss Florence," said Jane, hesitatingly, "would you mind borrowing some money of me? I've got ten dollars upstairs in my trunk, and I don't need it at all. It's proud I'll be to lend it to you."

"Thank you, Jane," said Florence, gratefully. "I thought I had but one friend. I find I have two -"

"Then you'll take the money? I'll go right up and get it."

"No, Jane; not at present. I have twenty dollars in my purse, and it will last me till I can earn more."

"But, miss, twenty dollars will soon go," said Jane, disappointed.

"If I find that I need the sum you so kindly offer me, I will let you know, I promise that."

"Thank you, miss."

At this point a bell rang from above.

"It's from Mr. Curtis' room," said Jane.

"Go and see what he wants."

Jane returned in a brief time with a note in her hand.

"Mr. Curtis asked me if you were still here," she explained, "and when I told him you were he asked me to give you this."

Florence took the note, and, opening it, read these lines:

> "Florence: Now that you have had time to think over your plan of leaving your old home, I hope you have come to see how foolish it is. Reflect that, if carried out, a life of poverty and squalid wretchedness amid homely and uncongenial surroundings awaits you; while, as my wife, you will live a life of luxury and high social position. There are many young ladies who would be glad to accept the chance which you so recklessly reject. By accepting my hand you will gratify our excellent uncle, and

make me the happiest of mortals. You will acquit me of mercenary motives, since you are now penniless, and your disobedience leaves me sole heir to Uncle John. I love you, and it will be my chief object, if you will permit it, to make you happy.

"Curtis Waring."

Florence ran her eyes rapidly over this note, but her heart did not respond, and her resolution was not shaken.

"Tell Mr. Waring there is no answer, Jane, if he inquires," she said.

"Was he tryin' to wheedle you into marryin' him?" asked Jane.

"He wished me to change my decision."

"I'm glad you've given him the bounce," said Jane, whose expressions were not always refined. "I wouldn't marry him myself."

Florence smiled. Jane was red haired, and her nose was what is euphemistically called *retrousse*. Even in her own circles she was not regarded as beautiful, and was hardly likely to lead a rich man to overlook her humble station, and sue for her hand.

"Then, Jane, you at least will not blame me for refusing my cousin's hand?"

"That I won't, miss. Do you know, Miss Florence" - and here Jane lowered her voice - "I've a suspicion that Mr. Curtis is married already?"

"What do you mean, Jane?" asked Florence, startled.

"There was a poor young woman called here last month and inquired for Mr. Curtis. She was very sorrowful-like, and poorly dressed. He came up when she was at the door, and he spoke harshlike, and told her to walk away with him. What they said I couldn't hear, but I've a suspicion that she was married to him, secretlike for I saw a wedding ring upon her finger."

"But, Jane, it would be base and infamous for him to ask for my hand when he was already married."

"I can't help it, miss. That's just what he wouldn't mind doin'. Oh, he's a sly deceiver, Mr. Curtis. I'd like to see him foolin' around me."

Jane nodded her head with emphasis, as if to intimate the kind of reception Curtis Waring would get if he attempted to trifle with her virgin affections.

"I hope what you suspect is not true," said Florence, gravely. "I do not like or respect Curtis, but I don't like to think he would be so base as that. If you ever see this young woman again, try to find out where she lives. I would like to make her acquaintance, and be a friend to her if she needs one."

"Shure, Miss Florence, you will be needin' a friend yourself."

"It is true, Jane. I forgot that I am no longer a young lady of fortune, but a penniless girl, obliged to work for a living."

"What would your uncle say if he knew that Mr. Curtis

had a wife?"

"We don't know that he has one, and till we do, it would not be honorable to intimate such a thing to Uncle John."

"Shure, he wouldn't be particular. It's all his fault that you're obliged to leave home, and go into the streets. Why couldn't he take no for an answer, and marry somebody else, if he can find anybody to have him?"

"I wish, indeed, that he had fixed his affections elsewhere," responded Florence, with a sigh.

"Shure, he's twice as old as you, Miss Florence, anyway."

"I shouldn't mind that so much, if that was the only objection."

"It'll be a great deal better marryin' a young man."

"I don't care to marry any one, Jane. I don't think I shall ever marry."

"It's all very well to say that, Miss Florence. Lots of girls say so, but they change their minds. I don't mean to live out always myself."

"Is there any young man you are interested in, Jane?"

"Maybe there is, and maybe there isn't, Miss Florence. If I ever do get married I'll invite you to the wedding."

"And I'll promise to come if I can. But I hear the bell. I think my friend Dodger has come."

"Shall I ask him in, miss?"

"No. Tell him I will be ready to accompany him at once."

She went out into the hall, and when the door was opened the visitor proved to be Dodger. He had improved his appearance so far as his limited means would allow. His hands and face were thoroughly clean; he had bought a new collar and necktie; his shoes were polished, and despite his shabby suit, he looked quite respectable. Getting a full view of him, Florence saw that his face was frank and handsome, his eyes bright, and his teeth like pearls.

"Shure, he's a great deal better lookin' than Mr. Curtis," whispered Jane. "Here, Mr. Dodger, take Miss Florence's valise, and mind you take good care of her."

"I will," answered Dodger, heartily. "Come, Miss Florence, if you don't mind walking over to Fourth Avenue, we'll take the horse cars."

So, under strange guidance, Florence Linden left her luxurious home, knowing not what awaited her. What haven of refuge she might find she knew not. She, like Dodger, was adrift in New York.

CHAPTER VIII

A FRIENDLY COMPACT

Florence, as she stepped on the sidewalk, turned, and fixed a last sad look on the house that had been her home for so many years. She had never anticipated such a sundering of home ties, and even now she found it difficult to realize that the moment had come when her life was to be rent in twain, and the sunlight of prosperity was to be darkened and obscured by a gloomy and uncertain future.

She had hastily packed a few indispensable articles in a valise which she carried in her hand.

"Let me take your bag, Miss Florence," said Dodger, reaching out his hand.

"I don't want to trouble you, Dodger."

"It ain't no trouble, Miss Florence. I'm stronger than you, and it looks better for me to carry it."

"You are very kind, Dodger. What would I do without you?"

"There's plenty that would be glad of the chance of helping you," said Dodger, with a glance of admiration at the fair face of his companion.

"I don't know where to find them," said Florence, sadly. "Even my uncle has turned against me."

"He's an old chump!" ejaculated Dodger, in a tone of disgust.

"Hush! I cannot hear a word against him. He has always been kind and considerate till now. It is the evil influence of my Cousin Curtis that has turned him against me. When he comes to himself I am sure he will regret his cruelty."

"He would take you back if you would marry your cousin."

"Yes; but that I will never do!" exclaimed Florence, with energy.

"Bully for you!" said Dodger. "Excuse me," he said, apologetically. "I ain't used to talkin' to young ladies, and perhaps that ain't proper for me to say."

"I don't mind, Dodger; your heart is in the right place."

"Thank you, Miss Florence. I'm glad you've got confidence in me. I'll try to deserve it."

"Where are we going?" asked the young lady, whose only thought up to this moment had been to get away from the presence of Curtis and his persecutions.

They had now reached Fourth Avenue, and a surface car was close at hand.

"We're going to get aboard that car," said Dodger, signaling with his free hand. "I'll tell you more when we're inside."

Florence entered the car, and Dodger, following, took a seat at her side.

They presented a noticeable contrast, for Florence was dressed as beseemed her station, while Dodger, in spite of his manly, attractive face, was roughly attired, and looked like a working boy.

When the conductor came along, he drew out a dime, and tendered it in payment of the double fare. The money was in the conductor's hand before Florence was fully aware.

"You must not pay for me, Dodger," she said.

"Why not?" asked the boy. "Ain't we friends?"

"Yes, but you have no money to spare. Here, let me return the money."

And she offered him a dime from her own purse.

"You can pay next time, Miss Florence. It's all right. Now, I'll tell you where we are goin'. A friend of mine, Mrs. O'Keefe, has a lodgin' house, just off the Bowery. I saw her last night, and she says she's got a good room that she can give you for two dollars a week - I don't know how much you'd be willing to pay, but -"

"I can pay that for a time at least. I have a little money, and I must find some work to do soon. Is this Mrs. O'Keefe a nice lady?"

"She ain't a lady at all," answered Dodger, bluntly. "She keeps an apple-stand near the corner of Bowery and Grand Street; but she's a good, respectable woman, and she's good-hearted. She'll be kind to you, and try to make things pleasant; but if you ain't satisfied -"

"It will do for the present. Kindness is what I need, driven as I am from the home of my childhood. But you, Dodger, where do you live?"

"I'm goin' to take a small room in the same house, Miss Florence."

"I shall be glad to have you near me."

"I am proud to hear you say that. I'm a poor boy, and you're a rich lady, but -"

"Not rich, Dodger. I am as poor as yourself."

"You're a reg'lar lady, anyway. You ain't one of my kind, but I'm going to improve and raise myself. I was readin' the other day of a rich man that was once a poor boy, and sold papers like me. But there's one thing in the way - I ain't got no eddication."

"You can read and write, can't you, Dodger?"

"Yes; I can read pretty well, but I can't write much."

"I will teach you in the evenings, when we are both at leisure."

"Will you?" asked the boy, with a glad smile. "You're very kind - I'd like a teacher like you."

"Then it's a bargain, Dodger," and Florence's face for the first time lost its sad look, as she saw an opportunity of helping one who had befriended her. "But you must promise to study faithfully."

"That I will. If I don't, I'll give you leave to lick me."

"I shan't forget that," said Florence, amused. "I will buy a ruler of good hard wood, and then you must look out. But, tell me, where have you lived hitherto?"

"I don't like to tell you, Miss Florence. I've lived ever since I was a kid with a man named Tim Bolton. He keeps a saloon on the Bowery, near Houston Street. It's a tough place, I tell you. I've got a bed in one corner - it's tucked away in a closet in the day."

"I suppose it is a drinking saloon?"

"Yes, that's what it is."

"And kept open very late?"

"Pretty much all night."

"Is this Tim Bolton any relation of yours?"

"He says he's my father; but I don't believe it."

"Have you always lived with him?"

"Ever since I was a small kid."

"Have you always lived in New York?"

"No; I was out in Australia. Tim was out in the country

part of the time, and part of the time he kept a saloon in Melbourne. There was thieves and burglars used to come into his place. I knew what they were, though they didn't think I did."

"How terrible for a boy to be subjected to such influences."

"But I've made up my mind I won't live with Tim no longer. I can earn my own livin' sellin' papers, or smashin' baggage, and keep away from Tim. I'd have done it before if I'd had a friend like you to care for me."

"We will stand by each other, Dodger. Heaven knows I need a friend, and if I can be a friend to you, and help you, I will."

"We'll get out here, Miss Florence. I told Mrs. O'Keefe I'd call at her stand, and she'll go over and show you your room."

They left the car at the corner of Grand Street, and Dodger led the way to an apple-stand, presided over by a lady of ample proportions, whose broad, Celtic face seemed to indicate alike shrewd good sense and a kindly spirit.

"Mrs. O'Keefe," said Dodger, "this is the young lady I spoke to you about - Miss Florence Linden."

"It's welcome you are, my dear, and I'm very glad to make your acquaintance. You look like a rale leddy, and I don't know how you'll like the room I've got for you."

"I cannot afford to be particular, Mrs. O'Keefe. I have had a - a reverse of circumstances, and I must be content with an humble home."

"Then I'll go over and show it to you. Here, Kitty, come and mind the stand," she called to a girl about thirteen across the street, "and don't let anybody steal the apples. Look out for Jimmy Mahone, he stole a couple of apples right under my nose this mornin', the young spalpeen!"

As they were crossing the street, a boy of fourteen ran up to Dodger.

"Dodger," said he, "you'd better go right over to Tim Bolton's. He's in an awful stew - says he'll skin you alive if you don't come to the s'loon right away."

CHAPTER IX

THE NEW HOME

"You can tell Tim Bolton," said Dodger, "that I don't intend to come back at all."

"You don't mean it, Dodger?" said Ben Holt, incredulously.

"Yes, I do. I'm going to set up for myself."

"Oh, Dodger," said Florence, "I'm afraid you will get into trouble for my sake!"

"Don't worry about that, Miss Florence. I'm old enough to take care of myself, and I've got tired of livin' with Tim."

"But he may beat you!"

"He'll have to get hold of me first."

They had reached a four-story tenement of shabby brick, which was evidently well filled up by a miscellaneous crowd of tenants; shop girls, mechanics, laborers and widows, living by their daily toil.

Florence had never visited this part of the city, and her

heart sank within her as she followed Mrs. O'Keefe through a dirty hallway, up a rickety staircase, to the second floor.

"One more flight of stairs, my dear," said Mrs. O'Keefe, encouragingly. "I've got four rooms upstairs; one of them is for you, and one for Dodger."

Florence did not reply. She began to understand at what cost she had secured her freedom from a distasteful marriage.

In her Madison Avenue home all the rooms were light, clean and luxuriously furnished. Here - But words were inadequate to describe the contrast.

Mrs. O'Keefe threw open the door of a back room about twelve feet square, furnished in the plainest manner, uncarpeted, except for a strip that was laid, like a rug, beside the bedstead.

There was a washstand, with a mirror, twelve by fifteen inches, placed above it, a pine bureau, a couple of wooden chairs, and a cane-seated rocking-chair.

"There, my dear, what do you say to that?" asked Mrs. O'Keefe, complacently. "All nice and comfortable as you would wish to see."

"It is - very nice," said Florence, faintly, sacrificing truth to politeness.

"And who do you think used to live here?" asked the apple-woman.

"I'm sure I don't know."

"The bearded woman in the dime museum," answered Mrs. O'Keefe, nodding her head. "She lived with me three months, and she furnished the room herself. When she went away she was hard up, and I bought the furniture of her cheap. You remember Madam Berger, don't you, Dodger?"

"Oh, yes, I seen her often."

"She got twenty-five dollars a week, and she'd ought to have saved money, but she had a good-for-nothin' husband that drank up all her hard earnin's."

"I hope she didn't drink herself," said Florence, who shuddered at the idea of succeeding a drunken tenant.

"Not a drop. She was a good, sober lady, if she did work in a dime museum. She only left here two weeks ago. It isn't every one I'd be willin' to take in her place, but I see you're a real leddy, let alone that Dodger recommends you. I hope you'll like the room, and I'll do all I can to make things pleasant. You can go into my room any hour, my dear, and do your little cookin' on my stove. I s'pose you'll do your own cookin'?"

"Well, not just at present," faltered Florence. "I am afraid I don't know much about cooking."

"You'll find it a deal cheaper, and it's more quiet and gentale than goin' to the eatin'-houses. I'll help you all I can, and glad to."

"Thank you, Mrs. O'Keefe, you are very kind," said Florence, gratefully. "Perhaps just at first you wouldn't object to taking me as a boarder, and letting me take my meals with you. I don't think I would like to go to the eating-houses alone."

"To be sure, my dear, if you wish it, and I'll be glad of your company. I'll make the terms satisfactory."

"I have no doubt of that," said Florence, feeling very much relieved.

"If I might be so bold, what kind of work are you going to do?"

"I hardly know. It has come upon me so suddenly. I shall have to do something, for I haven't got much money. What I should like best would be to write -"

"Is it for the papers you mean?"

"Oh, no; I mean for some author or lawyer."

"I don't know much about that," said Mrs. O'Keefe. "In fact, I don't mind tellin' you, my dear, that I can't write myself, but I earn a good livin' all the same by my apple-stand. I tell you, my dear," she continued in a confidential tone, "there is a good dale of profit in sellin' apples. It's better than sewin' or writin'. Of course, a young leddy like you wouldn't like to go into the business."

Florence shook her head, with a smile.

"No, Mrs. O'Keefe," she said. "I am afraid I haven't a business turn, and I should hardly like so public an employment."

"Lor', miss, it's nothin' if you get used to it. There's nothin' dull about my business, unless it rains, and you get used to havin' people look at you."

"It isn't all that are worth looking at like you, Mrs. O'Keefe," said Dodger, slyly.

"Oh, go away wid your fun, Dodger," said the apple-woman, good-naturedly. "I ain't much to look at, I know."

"I think there's a good deal of you to look at, Mrs. O'Keefe. You must weigh near three hundred."

"I've a good mind to box your ears, Dodger. I only weigh a hundred and ninety-five. But I can't be bothered wid your jokes. Can you sew, Miss Florence?"

"Yes; but I would rather earn my living some other way, if possible."

"Small blame to you for that. I had a girl in Dodger's room last year who used to sew for a livin'. Early and late she worked, poor thing, and she couldn't make but two dollars a week."

"How could she live?" asked Florence, startled, for she knew very little of the starvation wages paid to toiling women.

"She didn't live. She just faded away, and it's my belief the poor thing didn't get enough to eat. Every day or two I'd make an excuse to take her in something from my own table, a plate of meat, or a bit of toast and a cup of tay, makin' belave she didn't get a chance to cook for herself, but she got thinner and thinner, and her poor cheeks got hollow, and she died in the hospital at last."

The warm-hearted apple-woman wiped away a tear with the corner of her apron, as she thought of the poor girl whose sad fate she described.

"You won't die of consumption, Mrs. O'Keefe," said Dodger. "It'll take a good while for you to fade away."

"Hear him now," said the apple-woman, laughing. "He will have his joke, Miss Florence, but he's a good bye for all that, and I'm glad he's goin' to lave Tim Bolton, that ould thafe of the worruld."

"Now, Mrs. O'Keefe, you know you'd marry Tim if he'd only ask you."

"Marry him, is it? I'd lay my broom over his head if he had the impudence to ask me. When Maggie O'Keefe marries ag'in, she won't marry a man wid a red nose."

"Break it gently to him, Mrs. O'Keefe. Tim is just the man to break his heart for love of you."

Mrs. O'Keefe aimed a blow at Dodger, but he proved true to his name, and skillfully evaded it.

"I must be goin'," he said. "I've got to work, or I can't pay room rent when the week comes round."

"What are you going to do, Dodger?" asked Florence.

"It isn't time for the evenin' papers yet, so I shall go 'round to the piers and see if I can't get a job at smashin' baggage."

"But I shouldn't think any one would want to do that," said Florence, puzzled.

"It's what we boys call it. It's just carryin' valises and bundles. Sometimes I show strangers the way to Broadway. Last week an old man paid me a dollar to show him the way to the Cooper Institute. He was a gentleman, he was. I'd like to meet him ag'in. Good-by, Miss Florence; I'll be back some time this afternoon."

"And I must be goin', too," said Mrs. O'Keefe. "I can't depend on that Kitty; she's a wild slip of a girl, and just as like as not I'll find a dozen apples stole when I get back. I hope you won't feel lonely, my dear."

"I think I will lie down a while," said Florence. "I have a headache."

She threw herself on the bed, and a feeling of loneliness and desolation came over her.

Her new friends were kind, but they could not make up to her for her uncle's love, so strangely lost, and the home she had left behind.

CHAPTER X

THE ARCH CONSPIRATOR

In the house on Madison Avenue, Curtis Waring was left in possession of the field. Through his machinations Florence had been driven from home and disinherited.

He was left sole heir to his uncle's large property with the prospect of soon succeeding, for though only fifty-four, John Linden looked at least ten years older, and was as feeble as many men past seventy.

Yet, as Curtis seated himself at the breakfast table an hour after Florence had left the house, he looked far from happy or triumphant.

One thing he had not succeeded in, the conquest of his cousin's heart. Though he loved himself best, he was really in love with Florence, so far as he was capable of being in love with any one.

She was only half his age - scarcely that - but he persuaded himself that the match was in every way suitable.

He liked to fancy her at the head of his table, after the death of his uncle, which he anticipated in a few months at latest.

The more she appeared to dislike him, the more he determined to marry her, even against her will.

She was the only one likely to inherit John Linden's wealth, and by marrying her he would make sure of it.

Yet she had been willing to leave the home of her youth, to renounce luxury for a life of poverty, rather than to marry him.

When he thought of this his face became set and its expression stern and determined.

"Florence shall yet be mine," he declared, resolutely. "I will yet be master of her fate, and bend her to my will. Foolish girl, how dare she match her puny strength against the resolute will of Curtis Waring?"

"Was there any one else whom she loved?" he asked himself, anxiously. No, he could think of none. On account of his uncle's chronic invalidism, they had neither gone into society, nor entertained visitors, and in the midst of a great city Florence and her uncle had practically led the lives of recluses.

There had been no opportunity to meet young men who might have proved claimants for her hand.

"When did Miss Florence leave the house, Jane?" he inquired, as he seated himself at the table.

"Most an hour since," the girl answered, coldly, for she disliked Curtis as much as she loved and admired Florence.

"It is sad, very sad that she should be so headstrong," said Curtis, with hypocritical sorrow.

"It is sad for her to go away from her own uncle's house," returned Jane.

"And very - very foolish."

"I don't know about that, sir. She had her reasons," said Jane, significantly.

Curtis coughed.

He had no doubt that Florence had talked over the matter with her hand-maiden.

"Did she say where she was going, Jane?" he asked.

"I don't think the poor child knew herself, sir."

"Did she go alone?"

"No, sir; the boy that was here last night called for her."

"That ragamuffin!" said Curtis, scornfully. "She certainly shows extraordinary taste for a young lady of family."

"The boy seems a very kind and respectable boy," said Jane, who had been quite won by Dodger's kindness to her young mistress.

"He may be respectable, though I am not so sure of that; but his position in life is very humble. He is probably a bootblack; a singular person to select for the friend of a girl like Florence."

"There's them that stands higher that isn't half so good," retorted Jane, with more zeal than good grammar.

"Did Miss Florence take a cab?"

"No; she just walked."

"But she took some clothing with her?"

"She took a handbag - that is all. She will send for her trunk."

"If you find out where she is living, just let me know, Jane."

"I will if she is willing to have me," answered Jane, independently.

"Look here, Jane," said Curtis, angrily, "don't forget that you are not her servant, but my uncle's. It is to him you look for wages, not to Miss Florence."

"I don't need to be told that, sir. I know that well enough."

"Then you know that it is to him that your faithful services are due, not to Florence?"

"I'm faithful to both, Mr. Waring."

"You are aware that my uncle is justly displeased with my cousin?"

"I know he's displeased, but I am sure he has no good reason to be."

Curtis Waring bit his lips. The girl, servant as she was, seemed to be openly defying him. His imperious temper could ill brook this.

"Take care!" he said, with a frown. "You seem to be lacking in respect to me. You don't appear to understand my position in this house."

"Oh, yes, I do. I know you have schemed to get my poor young mistress out of the house, and have succeeded."

"I have a great mind to discharge you, girl," said Curtis, with lowering brow.

"I am not your servant, sir. You have nothing to do with me."

"You will see whether I have or not. I will let you remain for a time, as it is your attachment to Miss Florence that has made you forget yourself. You will find that it is for your interest to treat me respectfully."

A feeble step was heard at the door, and John Linden entered the breakfast-room. His face was sad, and he heaved a sigh as he glanced mechanically at the head of the table, where Florence usually sat.

Curtis Waring sprang to his feet, and placing himself at his uncle's side, led him to his seat.

"How do you feel this morning, uncle?" he asked, with feigned solicitude.

"Ill, Curtis. I didn't sleep well last night."

"I don't wonder, sir. You had much to try you."

"Is - is Florence here?"

"No, sir," answered Jane, promptly. "She left the house an hour ago."

A look of pain appeared on John Linden's pale face.

"Did - did she leave a message for me?" he asked, slowly.

"She asked me to bid you good-by for her," answered Jane, quickly.

"Uncle, don't let yourself be disturbed now with painful thoughts. Eat your breakfast first, and then we will speak of Florence."

John Linden ate a very light breakfast. He seemed to have lost his appetite and merely toyed with his food.

When he arose from the table, Curtis supported him to the library.

"It is very painful to me - this conduct of Florence's, Curtis," he said, as he sank into his armchair.

"I understand it fully, uncle," said Curtis. "When I think of it, it makes me very angry with the misguided girl."

"Perhaps I have been too harsh - too stern!"

"You, uncle, too harsh! Why, you are the soul of gentleness. Florence has shown herself very ungrateful."

"Yet, Curtis, I love that girl. Her mother seemed to live again in her. Have I not acted cruelly in requiring her to obey me or leave the house?"

"You have acted only for good. You are seeking her happiness."

"You really think this, Curtis?"

"I am sure of it."

"But how will it all end?" asked Linden, bending an anxious look upon his wily nephew.

"By Florence yielding."

"You are sure of that?"

"Yes. Listen, uncle; Florence is only capricious, like most girls of her age. She foolishly desires to have her own way. It is nothing more serious, I can assure you."

"But she has left the house. That seems to show that she is in earnest."

"She thinks, uncle, that by doing so she can bend you to her wishes. She hasn't the slightest idea of any permanent separation. She is merely experimenting upon your weakness. She expects you will recall her in a week, at the latest. That is all of it."

Like most weak men, it made Mr. Linden angry to have his strength doubted.

"You think that?" he said.

"I have no doubt of it."

"She shall find that I am resolute," he said, irritably. "I will not recall her."

"Bravo, uncle! Only stick to that, and she will yield unconditionally within a fortnight. A little patience, and you will carry your point. Then all will be smooth sailing."

"I hope so, Curtis. Your words have cheered me. I will be patient. But I hope I shan't have to wait long. Where is the morning paper?"

"I shall have to humor and deceive him," thought Curtis. "I shall have a difficult part to play, but I am sure to succeed at last."

CHAPTER XI

FLORENCE SECURES EMPLOYMENT

For a few days after being installed in her new home Florence was like one dazed.

She could not settle her mind to any plan of self-support.

She was too unhappy in her enforced exile from her home, and it saddened her to think that the uncle who had always been so kind was permanently estranged from her.

Though Mrs. O'Keefe was kind, and Dodger was her faithful friend, she could not accustom herself to her poor surroundings.

She had not supposed luxury so essential to her happiness.

It was worse for her because she had nothing to do but give way to her morbid fancies.

This Mrs. O'Keefe was clear-sighted enough to see.

"I am sorry to see you so downcast like, my dear young lady," she said.

"How can I help it, Mrs. O'Keefe?" returned Florence.

"Try not to think of your wicked cousin, my dear."

"It isn't of him that I think - it is of my uncle. How could he be so cruel, and turn against me after years of kindness?"

"It's that wicked Curtis that is settin' him against you, take my word for it, Miss Florence. Shure, he must be wake-minded to let such a spalpeen set him against a swate young leddy like you."

"He is weak in body, not in mind, Mrs. O'Keefe. You are right in thinking that it is Curtis that is the cause of my misfortune."

"Your uncle will come to his right mind some day, never fear! And now, my dear, shall I give you a bit of advice?"

"Go on, my kind friend. I will promise to consider whatever you say."

"Then you'd better get some kind of work to take up your mind - a bit of sewin', or writin', or anything that comes to hand. I suppose you wouldn't want to mind my apple-stand a couple of hours every day?"

"No," answered Florence. "I don't feel equal to that."

"It would do you no end of good to be out in the open air. It would bring back the roses to your pale cheeks. If you coop yourself up in this dark room, you'll fade away and get thin."

"You are right. I will make an effort and go out. Besides, I must see about work."

Here Dodger entered the room in his usual breezy way. In his hand he brandished a morning paper.

"How are you feelin', Florence?" he asked; he had given up saying Miss Florence at her request. "Here's an advertisement that'll maybe suit you."

"Show it to me, Dodger," said Florence, beginning to show some interest.

The boy directed her attention to the following advertisement:

> "Wanted. - A governess for a girl of twelve. Must be a good performer on the piano, and able to instruct in French and the usual English branches. Terms must be moderate. Apply to Mrs. Leighton, at 127 W.- Street."

"There, Florence, what do you say to that? That's better than sewin'."

"I don't know, Dodger, whether I am competent."

"You play on the pianner, don't you?"

"Yes."

"Well enough to teach?"

"I think so; but I may not have the gift of teaching."

"Yes, you have. Haven't you been teachin' me every

evenin'? You make everything just as clear as mud - no, I don't mean that. You just explain so that I can't help understandin'."

"Then," said Florence, "I suppose I am at liberty to refer to you."

"Yes; you can tell the lady to call at the office of Dodger, Esq., any mornin' after sunrise, and he'll give her full particulars."

Florence did not immediately decide to apply for the situation, but the more she thought of it the more she felt inclined to do so. The little experience she had had with Dodger satisfied her that she should enjoy teaching better than sewing or writing.

Accordingly, an hour later, she put on her street dress and went uptown to the address given in the advertisement.

No. 127 was a handsome brown-stone house, not unlike the one in which Florence had been accustomed to live. It was a refreshing contrast to the poor tenement in which she lived at present.

"Is Mrs. Leighton at home?" inquired Florence. "Yes, miss," answered the servant, respectfully. "Whom shall I say?"

"I have come to apply for the situation of governess," answered Florence, feeling rather awkward as she made the statement.

"Ah," said the servant, with a perceptible decline in respect. "Won't you step in?"

"Thank you."

"Well, she do dress fine for a governess," said Nancy to herself. "It's likely she'll put on airs."

The fact was that Florence was dressed according to her past social position - in a costly street attire - but it had never occurred to her that she was too well dressed for a governess.

She took her seat in the drawing-room, and five minutes later there was a rustling heard, and Mrs. Leighton walked into the room.

"Are you the applicant for the position of governess?" she asked, surveying the elegantly attired young lady seated on the sofa.

"Yes, Mrs. Leighton," answered Florence, easily, for she felt more at home in a house like this than in the tenement.

"Have you taught before?"

"Very little," answered Florence, smiling to herself, as she wondered what Mrs. Leighton would say if she could see Dodger, the only pupil she ever had. "However, I like teaching, and I like children."

"Pardon me, but you don't look like a governess, Miss -"

"Linden," suggested Florence, filling out the sentence. "Do governesses have a peculiar look?"

"I mean as to dress. You are more expensively dressed

than the average governess can afford."

"It is only lately that my circumstances required me to support myself. I should not be able to buy such a dress out of my present earnings."

"I am glad to hear you say that, for I do not propose to give a large salary."

"I do not expect one," said Florence, quietly. "You consider yourself competent to instruct in music, French and the English branches?"

"Oh, yes."

"Do you speak French?"

"Yes, madam."

"Would you favor me with a specimen of your piano playing?"

There was a piano in the back parlor. Florence removed her gloves, and taking a seat before it, dashed into a spirited selection from Strauss.

Mrs. Leighton listened with surprised approval.

"Certainly you are a fine performer," she said. "What - if I should engage you - would you expect in the way of compensation?"

"How much time would you expect me to give?"

"Three hours daily - from nine to twelve."

"I hardly know what to say. What did you expect to pay?"

"About fifty cents an hour."

Florence knew very well, from the sums that had been paid for her own education, that this was miserably small pay; but it was much more than she could earn by sewing.

"I will teach a month on those terms," she said, after a pause.

Mrs. Leighton looked well pleased. She knew that she was making a great bargain.

"Oh, by the way," she said, "can you give references?"

"I can refer you to Madam Morrison," naming the head of a celebrated female seminary. "She educated me."

"That will be quite satisfactory," said Mrs. Leighton, graciously. "Can you begin to-morrow?"

"Yes, madam."

"You will then see your pupil. At present she is out."

Florence bowed and withdrew.

She had been afraid Mrs. Leighton would inquire where she lived, and she would hardly dare to name the humble street which she called home.

She walked toward Fifth Avenue, when, just as she was turning the corner, she met Mr. Percy de

Brabazon, swinging a slender cane, and dressed in the extreme of the fashion.

"Miss Linden!" he exclaimed, eagerly. "This is - aw - indeed a pleasure. Where are you walking this fine morning? May I - aw - have the pleasure of accompanying you?"

Florence stopped short in deep embarrassment.

CHAPTER XII

A FRIEND, THOUGH A DUDE

Percy de Brabazon looked sincerely glad to meet Florence, and she herself felt some pleasure in meeting one who reminded her of her former life.

But it was quite impossible that she should allow him to accompany her to her poor home on the East Side.

"Thank you, Mr. de Brabazon, but my engagements this morning will hardly permit me to accept your escort," she said.

"I suppose that means that you are going shopping; but I don't mind it, I assure you, and I will carry your bundles," he added, magnanimously.

"That would never do. What! the fashionable Mr. de Brabazon carrying bundles? You would lose your social status."

"I don't mind, Miss Florence, as long as you give me - aw - an approving smile."

"I will give it now, as I bid you good-morning."

"May I - aw - have the pleasure of calling upon you

to-morrow evening, Miss Linden?"

"It is evident that you have not heard that I am no longer residing with my uncle."

Mr. de Brabazon looked surprised.

"No, I had not heard. May I ask - aw - where you are wesiding?"

"With friends," answered Florence, briefly. "As you are a friend and will be likely to hear it, I may as well mention that my uncle is displeased with me, and has practically disowned me."

"Then, Miss Florence," said Mr. de Brabazon, eagerly, "won't you accept - aw - my heart and hand? My mother will be charmed to receive you, and I - aw - will strive to make you happy."

"I appreciate your devotion, I do, indeed, Mr. de Brabazon," said Florence, earnestly; "but I must decline your offer. I will not marry without love."

"I don't mind that," said Percy, "if you'll agree to take a feller; you'll learn in time to like him a little. I am wich - I know you don't care for that - but I can give you as good a home as your uncle. If you would give me hope - aw -"

"I am afraid I cannot, Mr. de Brabazon, but if you will allow me to look upon you as a friend, I will call upon you if I have need of a friend's services."

"Will you, weally?"

"Yes, there is my hand on it. I ought to tell you that I must now earn my own living, and am to give lessons to a young pupil in West - Street, three hours daily."

"You don't mean to say you are actually poor?" said Mr. de Brabazon, horrified.

"Yes, indeed, I am."

"Then, won't you let me lend you some money? I've got more than I need, I have, 'pon my honor."

"Thank you, I promise to call upon you if I need it."

Mr. de Brabazon looked pleased.

"Would you mind telling me where you are going to teach, Miss Florence?"

Florence hesitated, but there was something so sincere and friendly in the young man's manner - dude though he was - that she consented to grant his request.

"I am to teach the daughter of Mr. Robert Leighton."

"Why, Miss Leighton is my cousin," said Percy, in joyous excitement.

"Indeed! Had I known that I would hardly have told you."

"Don't be afwaid! I will be vewy discreet," said Mr. De Brabazon.

"Thank you, and good-morning."

Florence went on her way, cheered and encouraged in spite of herself, by her success in obtaining employment, and by the friendly offers of Mr. de Brabazon.

"It is wrong to get discouraged," she said to herself. "After all, there are warm hearts in the world."

When she entered her humble home, she found Dodger already there. There was an eagerness in his manner, and a light in his eye, that seemed to indicate good news.

"Well, Dodger, what is it?"

"I've been waitin' half an hour to see you, Florence," he said. "I've got some work for you."

"What is it - sewing on a button, or mending a coat?"

"No, I mean workin' for money. You can play on the pianner, can't you?"

"Yes."

"They want a young lady to play the pianner at a dime museum, for nine dollars a week. It's a bully chance. I just told the manager - he's a friend of mine - that I had a young lady friend that was a stunnin' player, and he wants you to come around and see him."

It was a preposterous idea - so Florence thought - that she should consent to play at such a place; but she couldn't expect Dodger to look at the matter in the same light, so she answered, very gently and pleasantly:

"You are very kind, Dodger, to look out for me, but I shall not need to accept your friend's offer. I have secured a chance to teach uptown."

"You have? What'll you get?"

"I am to be employed three hours daily, at fifty cents an hour."

"Geewhillikens! that's good! You'd have to work as much as twelve hours at the museum for the same pay."

"You see, therefore, that I am provided for - that is, if I suit."

Dodger was a little disappointed. Still, he could not help admitting that it would be better for Florence to teach three hours, than to work ten or twelve. As to her having any objection to appearing at a dime museum, that never occurred to him.

Florence had sent for her trunk, and it was now in her room.

Dodger accompanied an expressman to the house, and luckily saw Jane, who arranged everything for him.

"How's the old gentleman?" asked Dodger. "Florence wanted me to ask."

"He's feeble," said Jane, shaking her head.

"Does he miss Florence?"

"That he do."

"Why don't he send for her, then, to come back?" asked Dodger, bluntly.

"Because Curtis Waring makes him believe she'll come around and ask forgiveness, if he only holds out. I tell you, Dodger, that Curtis is a viper."

"So he is," answered Dodger, who was not quite clear in his mind as to what a viper was. "I'd like to step on his necktie."

"If it wasn't for him, my dear young mistress would be back in the house within twenty-four hours."

"I don't see how the old gentleman can let him turn Florence out of the house."

"He's a snake in the grass, Dodger. It may be wicked, but I just wish something would happen to him. And how is Miss Florence lookin', poor dear?"

"She's lookin' like a daisy."

"Does she worry much?"

"She did at first, but now she's workin' every day, and she looks more cheerful-like."

"Miss Florence workin'! She that was always brought up like a lady!"

"She's teachin' a little girl three hours a day."

"Well, that isn't so bad!" said Jane, relieved. "Teachin' is genteel. I wish I could see her some day. Will you tell her, Dodger, that next Sunday is my day out, and

I'll be in Central Park up by the menagerie at three o'clock, if she'll only take the trouble to be up there?"

"I'll tell her, Jane, and I'm sure she'll be there."

A day or two afterward Curtis Waring asked: "Have you heard from my Cousin Florence since she went away?"

"Yes, sir."

"Indeed! Where is she staying?"

"She didn't send me word."

"How, then, did you hear from her?"

"Dodger came with an expressman for her trunk."

Curtis Waring frowned.

"And you let him have it?" he demanded, sternly.

"Of course I did. Why shouldn't I?"

"You should have asked me."

"And what business have you with Miss Florence's trunk, I'd like to know?" said Jane, independently.

"Never mind; you ought to have asked my permission."

"I didn't think you'd want to wear any of Miss Florence's things, Mr. Waring."

"You are silly and impertinent," said Curtis, biting his

lips. "Did that boy tell you anything about her?"

"Only that she wasn't worryin' any for you, Mr. Curtis."

Curtis glanced angrily at his cousin's devoted friend, and then, turning on his heel, left the room.

"I'll bring her to terms yet," he muttered. "No girl of seventeen shall defy me!"

CHAPTER XIII

TIM BOLTON'S SALOON

Not far from Houston Street, on the west side of the Bowery, is an underground saloon, with whose proprietor we are already acquainted.

It was kept by Tim Bolton, whose peculiar tastes and shady characteristics well fitted him for such a business.

It was early evening, and the gas jets lighted up a characteristic scene.

On the sanded floor were set several tables, around which were seated a motley company, all of them with glasses of beer or whiskey before them.

Tim, with a white apron on, was moving about behind the bar, ministering to the wants of his patrons. There was a scowl upon his face, for he was not fond of work, and he missed Dodger's assistance.

The boy understood the business of mixing drinks as well as he, and often officiated for hours at a time, thus giving his guardian and reputed father a chance to leave the place and meet outside engagements.

A tall, erect gentleman entered the saloon, and walked up to the bar.

"Good-evening, colonel," said Tim.

"Good-evening, sir," said the newcomer, with a stately inclination of the head.

He was really a colonel, having served in the Civil War at the head of a Georgia regiment.

He had all the stately courtesy of a Southern gentleman, though not above the weakness of a frequent indulgence in the strongest fluids dispensed by Tim Bolton.

"What'll you have, colonel?"

"Whiskey straight, sir. It's the only drink fit for a gentleman. Will you join me, Mr. Bolton?"

"Of course, I will," said Tim, as, pouring out a glass for himself, he handed the bottle to the colonel.

"Your health, sir," said the colonel, bowing.

"Same to you, colonel," responded Tim, with a nod.

"Where's the boy?"

Col. Martin had always taken considerable notice of Dodger, being naturally fond of boys, and having once had a son of his own, who was killed in a railroad accident when about Dodger's age.

"Danged if I know!" answered Tim, crossly.

"He hasn't left you, has he?"

"Yes; he's cleared out, the ungrateful young imp! I'd like to lay my hands on the young rascal."

"Was he your son?"

"He was my - stepson," answered Tim, hesitating.

"I see, you married his mother."

"Yes," said Tim, considering the explanation satisfactory, and resolved to adopt it. "I've always treated him as if he was my own flesh and blood, and I've raised him from a young kid. Now he's gone and left me."

"Can you think of any reason for his leaving you?"

"Not one. I always treated him well. He's been a great expense to me, and now he's got old enough to help me he must clear out. He's the most ungrateful cub I ever seen."

"I am sorry he has gone - I used to like to have him serve me."

"And now what's the consequence? Here I am tied down to the bar day and night."

"Can't you get some one in his place?"

"Yes, but I'd likely be robbed; I had a bartender once who robbed me of two or three dollars a day."

"But you trusted the boy?"

"Yes, Dodger wouldn't steal - I can say that much for him."

"There's one thing I noticed about the boy," said the colonel, reflectively. "He wouldn't drink. More than once I have asked him to drink with me, but he would always say, 'Thank you, colonel, but I don't like whiskey.' I never asked him to take anything else, for whiskey's the only drink fit for a gentleman. Do you expect to get the boy back?"

"If I could only get out for a day I'd hunt him up; but I'm tied down here."

"I seed him yesterday, Tim," said a red-nosed man who had just entered the saloon, in company with a friend of the same general appearance. Both wore silk hats, dented and soiled with stains of dirt, coats long since superannuated, and wore the general look of barroom loafers.

They seldom had any money, but lay in wait for any liberal stranger, in the hope of securing a free drink.

"Where did you see him, Hooker?" asked Tim Bolton, with sudden interest.

"Selling papers down by the Astor House."

"Think of that, colonel!" said Tim, disgusted. "Becomin' a common newsboy, when he might be in a genteel employment! Did you speak to him, Hooker?"

"Yes, I asked him if he had left you."

"What did he say?"

"That he had left you for good - that he was going to grow up respectable!"

"Think of that!" said Tim, with renewed disgust. "Did he say where he lived?"

"No."

"Did he ask after me?"

"No, except he said that you were no relation of his. He said he expected you stole him when he was a kid, and he hoped some time to find his relations."

Tim Bolton's face changed color, and he was evidently disturbed. Could the boy have heard anything? he wondered, for his suspicions were very near the truth.

"It's all nonsense!" he said, roughly. "Next time you see him, Hooker, foller him home, and find out where he lives."

"All right, Tim. It ought to be worth something," he insinuated, with a husky cough.

"That's so. What'll you take?"

"Whiskey," answered Hooker, with a look of pleased anticipation.

"You're a gentleman, Tim," he said, as he gulped down the contents of a glass without winking.

Briggs, his dilapidated companion, had been looking on in thirsty envy.

"I'll help Hooker to look for Dodger," he said.

"Very well, Briggs."

"Couldn't you stand a glass for me, too, Tim?" asked Briggs, eagerly.

"No," answered Bolton, irritably. "I've been at enough expense for that young rascal already."

But the colonel noticed the pathetic look of disappointment on the face of Briggs, and he was stirred to compassion.

"Drink with me, sir," he said, turning to the overjoyed Briggs.

"Thank you, colonel. You're a gentleman!"

"Two glasses, Tim."

So the colonel drained a second glass, and Briggs, pouring out with trembling fingers as much as he dared, followed suit.

When the last drop was drunk, he breathed a deep sigh of measureless enjoyment.

"If either of you bring that boy in here," said Tim, "I'll stand a couple of glasses for both."

"We're your men, Tim," said Hooker. "Ain't we, Briggs?"

"That's so, Hooker. Shake!"

And the poor victims of drink shook hands energetically. Long since they had sunk their manhood in the intoxicating cup, and henceforth lived only to gratify their unnatural craving for what would sooner or later bring them to a drunkard's grave.

As they left the saloon, the colonel turned to Tim, and said:

"I like whiskey, sir; but I'll be hanged if I can respect such men as those."

"They're bums, colonel, that's what they are!"

"How do they live?"

"Don't know. They're in here about every day."

"If it's drink that's brought them where they are, I'm half inclined to give it up; but, after all, it isn't necessary to make a beast of yourself. I always drink like a gentleman, sir."

"So you do, colonel."

At that moment a poor woman, in a faded calico dress with a thin shawl over her shoulders, descended the steps that led into the saloon, and walked up to the bar.

"Has my husband been here to-night?" she asked.

Tim Bolton frowned.

"Who's your husband?" he asked, roughly.

"Wilson."

"No, Bill Wilson hasn't been here to-night. Even if he had you have no business to come after him. I don't want any sniveling women here."

"I couldn't help it, Mr. Bolton," said the woman, putting her apron to her eyes. "If Bill comes in, won't you tell him to come home? The baby's dead, and we haven't a cent in the house!"

Even Tim was moved by this.

"I'll tell him," he said. "Take a drink yourself; you don't look strong. It shan't cost you a cent."

"No," said the woman, "not a drop! It has ruined my happiness, and broken up our home! Not a drop!"

"Here, my good lady," said the colonel, with chivalrous deference, "you have no money. Take this," and he handed the astonished woman a five-dollar bill.

"Heaven bless you, sir!" she exclaimed, fervently.

"Allow me to see you to the street," and the gallant Southern gentleman escorted her up to the sidewalk.

"I'd like to horsewhip that woman's husband. Don't you sell him another drop!" he said, when he returned.

CHAPTER XIV

THE MISSING WILL

An hour after the depart of the colonel there was an unexpected arrival.

A well-dressed gentleman descended the stairs gingerly, looked about him with fastidious disdain, and walked up to the bar.

Tim Bolton was filling an order, and did not immediately observe him.

When at length he turned around he exclaimed, in some surprise:

"Mr. Waring!"

"Yes, Bolton, I have found my way here."

"I have been expecting you."

"I came to you for some information."

"Well, ask your questions: I don't know whether I can answer them."

"First, where is my Cousin Florence?"

"How should I know? She wasn't likely to place herself under my protection."

"She's with that boy of yours - Dodger, I believe you call him. Where is he?"

"Run away," answered Bolton, briefly.

"Do you mean that you don't know where he is?"

"Yes, I do mean that. I haven't set my eyes on him since that night."

"What do you mean by such negligence? Do you remember who he is?"

"Certainly I do."

"Then why do you let him get of your reach?"

"How could I help it? Here I am tied down to this bar day and night! I'm nearly dead for want of sleep."

"It would be better to close up your place for a week and look after him."

"Couldn't do it. I should lose all my trade. People would say I was closed up."

"And have you done nothing toward his recovery?"

"Yes, I have sent out two men in search of him."

"Have you any idea where he is, or what he is doing?"

"Yes, he has been seen in front of the Astor House,

selling papers. I have authorized my agent, if he sees him again, to follow him home, and find out where he lives."

"That is good! Astor House? I may see him myself."

"But why do you want to see him? Do you want to restore him to his rights?"

"Hush!" said Curtis, glancing around him apprehensively. "What we say may be overheard and excite suspicion. One thing may be secured by finding him - the knowledge of Florence's whereabouts."

"What makes you think she and the boy are together?"

"He came for her trunk. I was away from home, or I would not have let it go -"

"It is strange that they two are together, considering their relationship."

"That is what I am afraid they will find out. She may tell him of the mysterious disappearance of her cousin, and he -"

"That reminds me," interrupted Bolton. "He told Hooker - Hooker was the man that saw him in front of the Astor House - that he didn't believe I was his father. He said he thought I must have stolen him when he was a young kid."

"Did he say that?" asked Curtis, in evident alarm.

"Yes, so Hooker says."

"If he has that idea in his head, he may put two and two together, and guess that he is the long-lost cousin of Florence. Tim, the boy must be got rid of."

"If you mean what I think you do, Mr. Waring, I'm not with you. I won't consent to harm the boy."

"You said that before. I don't mean anything that will shock your tender heart, Bolton," said Curtis, with a sneer. "I mean carried to a distance - Europe or Australia, for instance. All I want is to keep him out of New York till my uncle is dead. After that I don't care what becomes of him."

"That's better. I've no objection to that. How is the old gentleman?"

"He grieved so much at first over the girl's loss, that I feared he would insist on her being recalled at once. I soothed him by telling him that he had only to remain firm, and she would come around, and yield to his wishes."

"Do you think she will?" asked Tim, doubtfully.

"I intend she shall!" said Curtis, significantly. "Bolton, I love the girl all the more for her obstinate refusal to wed me. I have made up my mind to marry her with her consent, or without it."

"I thought it was only the estate you were after?"

"I want the estate and her with it. Mark my words, Bolton, I will have both!"

"You will have the estate, no doubt; Mr. Linden has

made his will in your favor, has he not?" and Bolton looked intently in the face of his visitor.

"Hark you, Bolton, there is a mystery I cannot fathom. My uncle made two wills. In the earlier, he left the estate to Florence and myself, if we married; otherwise, to me alone."

"That is satisfactory."

"Yes, but there was another, in which the estate goes to the son, if living. That will has disappeared."

"Is it possible?" asked Bolton, in astonishment. "When was it missed?"

"On the night of the burglary."

"Then you think -"

"That the boy, Dodger, has it. Good Heavens! if he only knew that by this will the estate goes to him!" and Waring wiped the perspiration from his brow.

"You are sure he did not give you the will?" he demanded, eying Bolton sharply.

"I have not seen him since the night of the robbery."

"If he has read the will, it may lead to dangerous suspicions."

"He would give it to your cousin, Florence, would he not?"

"Perhaps so. Bolton, you must get the boy back, and

take the will from him, if you can."

"I will do my best; but you must remember that Dodger is no longer a small kid. He is a boy of eighteen, strong and well grown. He wouldn't be easy to manage. Besides, as long as he doesn't know that he has any interest in the will, his holding it won't do any harm. Is the old gentleman likely to live long?"

"I don't know. I sometimes hope - Pshaw! why should I play the hypocrite when speaking to you? Surely it is no sin to wish him better off, since he can't enjoy life!"

"He might if Florence and his son were restored to him."

"What do you mean, Bolton?" asked Curtis, suspiciously.

"What could I mean? It merely occurred to me," said Bolton, innocently. "You say he is quiet, thinkin' the girl will come around?"

"Yes."

"Suppose time passes, and she doesn't? Won't he try to find her? As she is in the city, that won't be hard."

"I shall represent that she has left the city."

"For any particular point?"

"No, that is not necessary."

"And then?"

"If he worries himself into the grave, so much the

better for me."

"There is no halfway about you, Mr. Curtis Waring."

"Why should there be? Listen, Bolton; I have set my all on this cast. I am now thirty-six, and still I am dependent upon my uncle's bounty. I am in debt, and some of my creditors are disposed to trouble me. My uncle is worth - I don't know how much, but I think half a million. What does he get out of it? Food and clothes, but not happiness. If it were mine, all the avenues of enjoyment would be open to me. That estate I must have."

"Suppose you get it, what is there for me?" asked Bolton.

"I will see that you are recompensed if you help me to it."

"Will you put that in writing?"

"Do you take me for a fool? To put it in writing would be to place me in your power! You can trust me."

"Well, perhaps so," said Tim Bolton, slowly.

"At any rate you will have to. Well, good-night. I will see you again. In the meantime try to find the boy."

Tim Bolton followed him with his eyes, as he left the saloon.

"What would he say," said Bolton to himself, "if he knew that the will he so much wishes to find is in my hands, and that I hold him in my power already?"

CHAPTER XV

THE NEW GOVERNESS

"Wish me luck, Dodger!"

"So I do, Florence. Are you goin' to begin teachin' this mornin'?"

"Yes; and I hope to produce a favorable impression. It is very important to me to please Mrs. Leighton and my future pupil."

"I'm sure you'll suit. How nice you look!"

Florence smiled, and looked pleased. She had taken pains with her dress and personal appearance, and, being luckily well provided with handsome dresses, had no difficulty in making herself presentable. As she stepped out of the shabby doorway upon the sidewalk no one supposed her to be a tenant, but she was generally thought to be a visitor, perhaps the agent of some charitable association.

"Perhaps all will not judge me as favorably as you do, Dodger," said Florence, with a laugh.

"If you have the headache any day, Florence, I'll take your place."

"You would look rather young for a tutor, Dodger, and I am afraid you would not be dignified. Good-morning! I shall be back to dinner."

"I am glad to find you punctual, Miss Linden," said Mrs. Leighton, as Florence was ushered into her presence. "This is your pupil, my daughter, Carrie."

Florence smiled and extended her hand.

"I hope we will like each other," she said.

The little girl eyed her with approval. This beautiful young lady was a pleasant surprise to her, for, never having had a governess, she expected to meet a stiff, elderly lady, of stern aspect. She readily gave her hand to Florence, and looked relieved.

"Carrie," said Mrs. Leighton, "you may show Miss Linden the way to the schoolroom."

"All right, mamma," and the little girl led the way upstairs to a back room on the third floor.

"So this is to be our schoolroom, is it, Carrie?" said Florence. "It is a very pleasant room."

"Yes; but I should have preferred the front chamber. Mamma thought that I might be looking into the street too much. Here there is only a back yard, and nothing to look at."

"Your mamma seems very judicious," said Florence, smiling. "Are you fond of study?"

"Well, I ain't exactly fond, but I will do my best."

"That is all that can be expected."

"Do you know, Miss Linden, you don't look at all like I expected."

"Am I to be glad or sorry for that?"

"I thought you would be an old maid, stiff and starched, like May Robinson's governess."

"I am not married, Carrie, so perhaps you may regard me as an old maid."

"You'll never be an old maid," said Carrie, confidently. "You are too young and pretty."

"Thank you, Carrie," said Florence, with a little blush. "You say that, I hope, because you are going to like me."

"I like you already," said the little girl, impulsively. "I've got a cousin that will like you, too."

"A young girl?"

"No; of course not. He is a young man. His name is Percy de Brabazon. It is a funny name, isn't it? You see, his father was a Frenchman."

Florence was glad that she already knew from Percy's own mouth of the relationship, as it saved her from showing a degree of surprise that might have betrayed her acquaintance with the young man.

"What makes you think your cousin would like me, Carrie?"

"Because he always likes pretty girls. He is a masher."

"That's slang, Carrie. I am sure your mamma wouldn't approve your using such a word."

"Don't tell her. It just slipped out. But about Percy - he wants very much to be married."

Florence was not surprised to hear this, for she had the best reason for knowing it to be true.

"Is he a handsome young man?" she asked, demurely.

"He's funny looking. He's awful good-natured, but he isn't the sort of young man I would like," concluded Carrie, with amusing positiveness.

"I hope you don't let your mind run on such things. You are quite too young."

"Oh, I don't think much about it. But Percy is a dude. He spends a sight for clothes. He always looks as if he had just come out of a bandbox."

"Is he in any business?"

"No; he has an independent fortune, so mamma says. He was in Europe last year."

"I think, Carrie, we must give up talking and attend to business. I should have checked you before, but I thought a little conversation would help us to get acquainted. Now show me your books, and I will assign your lessons."

"Don't give me too long lessons, please, Miss Linden."

"I will take care not to task you beyond your strength. I don't want my pupil to grow sick on my hands."

"I hope you won't be too strict. When May Robinson makes two mistakes her governess makes her learn her lessons over again."

"I will promise not to be too strict. Now let me see your books."

The rest of the forenoon was devoted to study.

Florence was not only an excellent scholar, but she had the art of imparting knowledge, and, what is very important, she was able in a few luminous words to explain difficulties and make clear what seemed to her pupil obscure.

So the time slipped quickly and pleasantly away, and it was noon before either she or her pupil realized it.

"It can't be twelve," said Carrie, surprised.

"Yes, it is. We must defer further study till to-morrow."

"Why, it is a great deal pleasanter than going to school, Miss Linden. I dreaded studying at home, but now I like it."

"I hope you will continue to, Carrie. I can say that the time has passed away pleasantly for me."

As Florence prepared to resume her street dress, Carrie said:

"Oh, I forgot! Mamma asked me to invite you to stay

to lunch with me. I take lunch as soon as school is out, at twelve o'clock, so I won't detain you long."

"Thank you, Carrie; I will stay with pleasure."

"I am glad of that, for I don't like to sit down to the table alone. Mamma is never here at this time. She goes out shopping or making calls, so poor I have to sit down to the table alone. It will be ever so much pleasure to have you with me."

Florence was by no means sorry to accept the invitation.

The meals she got at home were by no means luxurious, and the manner of serving them was by no means what she enjoyed.

Mrs. O'Keefe, though a good friend and a kindhearted woman, was not a model housekeeper, and Florence had been made fastidious by her early training. Lunch was, of course, a plain meal, but what was furnished was of the best quality, and the table service was such as might be expected in a luxurious home.

Just as Florence was rising from the table, Mrs. Leighton entered the room in street dress.

"I am glad you remained to lunch, Miss Linden," she said. "You will be company for my little girl, who is very sociable. Carrie, I hope you were a good girl, and gave Miss Linden no trouble."

"Ask Miss Linden, mamma," said Carrie, confidently.

"Indeed, she did very well," said Florence. "I foresee

that we shall get along admirably."

"I am glad to hear that. She is apt to be indolent."

"I won't be with Miss Linden, mamma. She makes the studies so interesting."

After Florence left the house, Carrie pronounced an eulogium upon her which led Mrs. Leighton to congratulate herself upon having secured a governess who had produced so favorable an impression on her little girl.

"Was you kept after school, Florence?" asked Dodger, as she entered her humble home. "I am afraid you'll find your dinner cold."

"Never mind, Dodger. I am to take dinner - or lunch, rather - at the house where I am teaching; so hereafter Mrs. O'Keefe need not wait for me."

"And how do you like your place?"

"It is everything that is pleasant. You wished me good luck, Dodger, and your wish has been granted."

"I was lucky, too, Florence. I've made a dollar and a quarter this mornin'."

"Not by selling papers, surely?"

"Not all. A gentleman gave me fifty cents for takin' his valise to the Long Branch boat."

"It seems we are both getting rich," said Florence, smiling.

CHAPTER XVI

DODGER BECOMES AMBITIOUS

"Ah, there, Dodger!"

Dodger, who had been busily and successfully selling evening papers in front of the Astor House, turned quickly as he heard his name called.

His glance rested on two men, dressed in soiled white hats and shabby suits, who were apparently holding each other up, having both been imbibing.

He at once recognized Hooker and Briggs, for he had waited upon them too many times in Tim's saloon not to recognize them.

"Well," he said, cautiously, "what do you want?"

"Tim has sent us for you!" answered the two, in unison.

"What does he want of me?"

"He wants you to come home. He says he can't get along without you."

"He will have to get along without me," said the boy,

independently. "Tell him I'm not goin' back!"

"You're wrong, Dodger," said Hooker, shaking his head, solemnly. "Ain't he your father?"

"No, he ain't."

"He says he is," continued Hooker, looking puzzled.

"That don't make it so."

"He ought to know," put in Briggs.

"Yes; he ought to know!" chimed in Hooker.

"No doubt he does, but he can't make me believe he's any relation of mine."

"Just go and argy the point with him," said Hooker, coaxingly.

"It wouldn't do no good."

"Maybe it would. Just go back with us, that's a good boy."

"What makes you so anxious about it?" asked Dodger, suspiciously.

"Well," said Hooker, coughing, "we're Tim's friends, don't you know."

"What's he goin' to give you if I go back with you?" asked the boy, shrewdly.

"A glass of whiskey!" replied Hooker and Briggs

in unison.

"Is that all?"

"Maybe he'd make it two."

"I won't go back with you," said Dodger, after a moment's thought; "but I don't want you to lose anything by me. Here's a dime apiece, and you can go and get a drink somewhere else."

"You're a trump, Dodger," said Hooker, eagerly holding out his hand.

"I always liked you, Dodger," said Briggs, with a similar motion.

"Now, don't let Tim know you've seen me," said the newsboy, warningly.

"We won't."

And the interesting pair ambled off in the direction of the Bowery.

"So Tim sent them fellers after me?" soliloqized Dodger. "I guess I'll have to change my office, or maybe Tim himself will be droppin' down on me some mornin'. It'll be harder to get rid of him than of them chumps."

So it happened that he used to take down his morning papers to the piers on the North River, and take his chance of selling them to passengers from Boston and others ports arriving by the Fall River boats, and others from different points.

The advantage of this was that he often got a chance to serve as guide to strangers visiting the city for the first time, or as porter, to carry their valise or other luggage.

Being a bright, wideawake boy, with a pleasant face and manner, he found his services considerably in demand; and on counting up his money at the end of the week, he found, much to his encouragement, that he had received on an average about a dollar and twenty-five cents per day.

"That's better than sellin' papers alone," thought he. "Besides, Tim isn't likely to come across me here. I wonder I didn't think of settin' up for myself before!"

In the evening he spent an hour, and sometimes more, pursuing his studies, under the direction of Florence. At first his attention was given chiefly to improving his reading and spelling, for Dodger was far from fluent in the first, while his style of spelling many words was strikingly original.

"Ain't I stupid, Florence?" he asked one day, after spelling a word of three syllables with such ingenious incorrectness as to convulse his young teacher with merriment.

"Not at all, Dodger. You are making excellent progress; but sometimes you are so droll that I can't help laughing."

"I don't mind that if you think I am really gettin' on."

"Undoubtedly you are!"

"I make a great many mistakes," said Dodger, dubiously.

"Yes, you do; but you must remember that you have taken lessons only a short time. Don't you think you can read a good deal more easily than you did?"

"Yes; I don't trip up half so often as I did. I'm afraid you'll get tired of teachin' me."

"No fear of that, Dodger. As long as I see that you are improving, I shall feel encouraged to go on."

"I wish I knew as much as your other scholar."

"You will in time if you go on. You mustn't get discouraged."

"I won't!" said Dodger, stoutly. "If a little gal like her can learn, I'd ought to be ashamed if I don't - a big boy of eighteen."

"It isn't the size of the boy that counts, Dodger."

"I know that, but I ain't goin' to give in, and let a little gal get ahead of me!"

"Keep to that determination, Dodger, and you will succeed in time, never fear."

On the whole, Florence enjoyed both her pupils. She had the faculty of teaching, and she became very much interested in both.

As for Dodger, she thought, rough diamond as he was, that she saw in him the making of a manly man, and she felt that it was a privilege to assist in the development of his intellectual nature.

Again, he had picked up a good deal of slang from the nature of his associates, and she set to work to improve his language, and teach him refinement.

It was necessarily a slow process, but she began to find after a time that a gradual change was coming over him.

"I want you to grow up a gentleman, Dodger," she said to him one day.

"I'm too rough for that, Florence. I'm only an ignorant street boy."

"You are not going to be an ignorant street boy all your life. I don't see why you should not grow up a polished gentleman."

"I shall never be like that de Brabazon young man," said he.

"No, Dodger; I don't think you will," said Florence, laughing. "I don't want you to become effeminate nor a dude. I think I would like you less than I do now."

"Do you like me, Florence?" asked Dodger, brightening up.

"To be sure I do. I hope you don't doubt it."

"Why, it don't seem natural-like. You're a fashionable young lady -"

"Not very fashionable, Dodger, just at present."

"Well, a high-toned young lady - one of the tip-tops,

and I am a rough Bowery boy."

"You were once, but you are getting over that rapidly. Did you ever hear of Andy Johnson?"

"Who was he?"

"He became President of the United States. Well, at the age of twenty-one he could neither read nor write."

"At twenty-one?" repeated Dodger. "Why, I'm only eighteen, and I do know something of readin' and writin'."

"To be sure! Well, Andy Johnson was taught to read and write by his wife. He kept on improving himself till, in course of time, he became a United States Senator, Vice-President, and afterward, President. Now, I don't expect you to equal him, but I see no reason why you should not become a well-educated man if you are content to work, and keep on working."

"I will keep on, Florence," said Dodger, earnestly.

"If I ever find my relations I don't want them to be ashamed of me."

It was not the first time he had referred to his uncertain origin.

"Won't Tim Bolton tell you anything about your family?"

"No; I've asked him more'n once. He always says he's my father, and that makes me mad."

"It is strange," said Florence, thoughtfully. "I had a young cousin stolen many years ago."

"Was it the son of the old gentleman you lived with on Madison Avenue?"

"Yes; it was the son of Uncle John. It quite broke him down. After my cousin's loss he felt that he had nothing to live for."

"I wish I was your cousin, Florence," said Dodger, thoughtfully.

"Well, then, I will adopt you as my cousin, or brother, whichever you prefer!"

"I would rather be your cousin."

"Then cousin let it be! Now we are bound to each other by strong and near ties."

"But when your uncle takes you back you'll forget all about poor Dodger."

"No, I won't, Dodger. There's my hand on it. Whatever comes, we are friends forever."

"Then I'll try not to disgrace you, Florence. I'll learn as fast as I can, and see if I don't grow up to be a gentleman."

CHAPTER XVII

A MYSTERIOUS ADVENTURE

Several weeks passed without changing in any way the position or employment of Dodger or Florence.

They had settled down to their respective forms of labor, and were able not only to pay their modest expenses, but to save up something for a rainy day.

Florence had but one source of regret.

She enjoyed her work, and did not now lament the luxurious home which she had lost.

But she did feel sore at heart that her uncle made no sign of regret for their separation.

From him she received no message of forgiveness or reconciliation.

"He has forgotten me!" she said to herself, bitterly. "He has cast me utterly out of his heart. I do not care for his money, but I do not like to think that my kind uncle - for he was always kind till the last trouble - has steeled his heart against me forever."

But she learned through a chance meeting with Jane,

that this was not so.

"Mr. Linden is getting very nervous and low-spirited," said the girl, "and sits hour after hour in the library looking into the fire, a-fotchin' deep sighs every few minutes. Once I saw him with your photograph - the one you had taken last spring - in his hands, and he looked sad-like when he laid it down."

"My dear uncle! Then he does think of me some-times?"

"It's my belief he'd send for you if Curtis would let him."

"Surely Curtis cannot exercise any restraint upon him?"

"He has frequent talks with the old gentleman. I don't know what he says, but it's sure to be something wicked. I expect he does all he can to set him against you. Oh, he's a cunning villain, he is, even if he is your cousin, Miss Florence."

"And do you think my uncle is unhappy, Jane?" said Florence, thoughtfully.

"That I do, miss."

"He never was very bright or cheerful, you know."

"But he never was like this. And I do think he's gettin' more and more feeble."

"Do you think I ought to call upon him, and risk his sending me away?"

"It might be worth tryin', Miss Florence."

The result of this conversation was that Florence did make up her mind the very next afternoon to seek her old home. She had just reached the front steps, and was about to ascend, when the door opened and Curtis appeared.

He started at sight of his cousin.

"Florence!" he said. "Tell me why you came here?"

"I am anxious about my uncle," she said. "Tell me, Curtis, how he is."

"You know he's never in vigorous health," said Curtis, evasively.

"But is he as well as usual?"

"He is about the same as ever. One thing would do more for him than anything else."

"What's that?"

"Your agreement to marry me," and he fixed his eyes upon her face eagerly.

Florence shook her head.

"I should be glad to help my uncle," she said, "but I cannot agree to marry you."

"Why not?" he demanded, roughly.

"Because I do not love you, and never shall," she

responded, firmly.

"In other words, you refuse to do the only thing that will restore our uncle to health and happiness?"

"It is too much to ask." Then, fixing her eyes upon him keenly: "Why should uncle insist upon this marriage? Is it not because you have influenced him in the matter?"

"No," answered Curtis, falsely. "He has some secret reason, which he will not disclose to me, for desiring it."

Florence had learned to distrust the words of her wily cousin.

"May I not see him?" she asked. "Perhaps he will tell me."

"No; I cannot permit it."

"You cannot permit it? Are you, then, our uncle's guardian?"

"No, and yes. I do not seek to control him, but I wish to save him from serious agitation. Should he see you, and find that you are still rebellious, the shock might kill him."

"I have reason to doubt your words," said Florence, coldly. "I think you are resolved to keep us apart."

"Listen, and I will tell you a secret; Uncle John has heart disease, so the doctor assures me. Any unwonted agitation might kill him instantly. I am sure you would not like to expose him to such a risk."

He spoke with apparent sincerity, but Florence did not feel certain that his words were truthful.

"Very well," she said. "Then I will give up seeing him."

"It is best, unless you are ready to accede to his wishes - and mine."

She did not answer, but walked away slowly.

"It would never do to have them meet!" muttered Curtis. "The old gentleman would ask her to come back on any terms, and then all my scheming would be upset. That was a happy invention of mine, about heart disease," he continued, with a low laugh. "Though she only half believed it, she will not dare to run the risk of giving him a shock."

It was about this time that the quiet tenor of Dodger's life was interrupted by a startling event.

He still continued to visit the piers, and one afternoon about six o'clock, he stood on the pier awaiting the arrival of the day boat from Albany, with a small supply of evening papers under his arm.

He had sold all but half a dozen when the boat touched the pier. He stood watching the various passengers as they left the boat and turned their steps in different directions, when some one touched him on the shoulder.

Looking up, he saw standing at his side a man of

slender figure, with gray hair and whiskers.

"Boy," he said, "I am a stranger in the city. Can I ask your assistance?"

"Yes, sir; certainly," answered Dodger, briskly.

"Do you know where the nearest station of the elevated road is?"

"Yes, sir?"

"I want to go uptown, but I know very little about the city. Will you accompany me as guide? I will pay you well."

"All right, sir," answered Dodger.

It was just the job he was seeking.

"We will have to walk a few blocks, unless you want to take a carriage."

"It isn't necessary. I am strong, in spite of my gray hair."

And indeed he appeared to be.

Dodger noticed that he walked with the elastic step of a young man, while his face certainly showed no trace of wrinkles.

"I live in the West," said the stranger, as they walked along. "I have not been here for ten years."

"Then you have never ridden on the elevated road?"

said Dodger.

"N-no," answered the stranger, with curious hesitation.

Yet when they reached the station he went up the staircase and purchased his ticket with the air of a man who was thoroughly accustomed to doing it.

"I suppose you don't want me any longer," said Dodger, preparing to resign the valise he was carrying, and which, by the way, was remarkably light considering the size.

"Yes, I shall need you," said the other hurriedly. "There may be some distance to walk after we get uptown."

"All right, sir."

Dodger was glad that further service was required, for this would of course increase the compensation which he would feel entitled to ask.

They entered one of the cars, and sat down side by side.

The old gentleman drew a paper from his pocket, and began to read, while Dodger, left to his own devices, sat quiet and looked about him.

He was rather surprised that the old gentleman, who, according to his own representation, was riding upon the elevated road for the first time, seemed to feel no curiosity on the subject, but conducted himself in all respects like an experienced traveler.

"He's a queer customer!" thought Dodger. "However, it's all one to me, as long as he pays me well for the job."

They got out at One Hundred and Twenty-fifth Street, and struck down toward the river, Dodger carrying the valise.

"I wonder where we're going?" he asked himself.

At length they reached a wooden house of three stories, standing by itself, and here the stranger stopped.

He rang the bell, and the door was opened by a hump-backed negro, who looked curiously at Dodger.

"Is the room ready, Julius?" asked the old man.

"Yes, sir."

"Boy, take the valise upstairs, and I will follow you."

Up two flights of stairs walked Dodger, followed by the old man and the negro.

The latter opened the door of a back room, and Dodger, obedient to directions, took the valise inside and deposited it on a chair.

He had hardly done so when the door closed behind him, and he heard the slipping of a bolt.

"What does all this mean?" Dodger asked himself in amazement.

CHAPTER XVIII

IN A TRAP

"Hold on there! Open that door!" he exclaimed, aloud.

There was no answer.

"I say, let me out!" continued our hero, beginning to kick at the panels.

This time there was an answer.

"Stop that kicking, boy! I will come back in fifteen minutes and explain all."

"Well," thought Dodger, "this is about the strangest thing that ever happened to me. However, I can wait fifteen minutes."

He sat down on a cane chair - there were two in the room - and looked about him.

He was in an ordinary bedroom, furnished in the usual manner. There was nothing at all singular in its appearance.

On a book shelf were a few books, and some old numbers of magazines. There was one window looking into a back yard, but as the room was small it was sufficient to light the apartment.

Dodger looked about in a cursory manner, not feeling any particular interest in his surroundings, for he had but fifteen minutes to wait, but he thought it rather queer that it should be thought necessary to lock him in.

He waited impatiently for the time to pass.

Seventeen minutes had passed when he heard the bolt drawn. Fixing his eyes eagerly on the door he saw it open, and two persons entered.

One was the hump-backed negro, carrying on a waiter a plate of buttered bread, and a cup of tea; the other person was - not the old man, but, to Dodger's great amazement, a person well-remembered, though he had only seen him once - Curtis Waring.

"Set down the waiter on the table, Julius," said Waring.

Dodger looked on in stupefaction. He was getting more and more bewildered.

"Now, you can go!" said Curtis, in a tone of authority.

The negro bowed, and after he had disposed of the waiter, withdrew.

"Do you know me, boy?" asked Curtis, turning now and addressing Dodger.

"Yes; you are Mr. Waring."

"You remember where you last saw me?"

"Yes, sir. At your uncle's house on Madison Avenue."

"Quite right."

"How did you come here? Where is the old man whose valise I brought from the Albany boat?"

Curtis smiled, and drew from his pocket a gray wig and whiskers.

"You understand now, don't you?"

"Yes, sir; I understand that I have been got here by a trick."

"Yes," answered Curtis, coolly. "I have deemed it wise to use a little stratagem. But you must be hungry. Sit down and eat your supper while I am talking to you."

Dodger was hungry, for it was past his usual supper time, and he saw no reason why he should not accept the invitation.

Accordingly, he drew his chair up to the table and began to eat. Curtis seated himself on the other chair.

"I have a few questions to ask you, and that is why I arranged this interview. We are quite by ourselves," he added, significantly.

"Very well, sir; go ahead."

"Where is my Cousin Florence? I am right, I take it, in assuming that you know where she is."

"Yes, sir; I know," answered Dodger, slowly.

"Very well, tell me."

"I don't think she wants you to know."

Curtis frowned.

"It is necessary I should know!" he said, emphatically.

"I will ask her if I may tell you."

"I can't wait for that. You must tell me at once."

"I can't do that."

"You are mistaken; you can do it."

"Then, I won't!" said Dodger, looking his companion full in the face.

Curtis Waring darted a wicked look at him, and seemed ready to attack the boy who was audacious enough to thwart him, but he restrained himself and said:

"Let that pass for the present. I have another question to ask. Where is the document you took from my uncle's desk on the night of the burglary?"

And he emphasized the last word.

Dodger looked surprised.

"I took no paper," he said.

"Do you deny that you opened the desk?" asked Curtis.

"No."

"When I came to examine the contents in the presence of my uncle, it was found that a document - his will - had disappeared, and with it a considerable sum of money."

And he looked sharply at Dodger.

"I don't know anything about it, sir. I took nothing."

"You can hardly make me believe that. Why did you open the desk if you did not propose to take anything?"

"I did intend to take something. I was under orders to do so, for I wouldn't have done it of my own free will; but the moment I got the desk open I heard a cry, and looking around, I saw Miss Florence looking at me."

"And then?"

"I was startled, and ran to her side."

"And then you went back and completed the robbery?"

"No, I didn't. She talked to me so that I felt ashamed of it. I never stole before, and I wouldn't have tried to do it then, if - if some one hadn't told me to."

"I know whom you mean - Tim Bolton."

"Yes, Tim Bolton, since you know."

"What did he tell you to take?"

"The will and the money."

"Eactly. Now we are coming to it. You took them, and gave them to him?"

"No, I didn't. I haven't seen him since that night."

Curtis Waring regarded the boy thoughtfully. His story was straightforward, and it agreed with the story told by Tim himself. But, on the other hand, he denied taking the missing articles, and yet they had disappeared.

Curtis decided that both he and Tim had lied, and that this story had been concocted between them.

Probably Bolton had the will and the money - the latter he did not care for - and this thought made him uneasy, for he knew that Tim Bolton was an unscrupulous man, and quite capable of injuring him, if he saw the way clear to do so.

"My young friend," he said, "your story is not even plausible. The articles are missing, and there was no one but yourself and Florence who were in a position to take them. Do you wish me to think that my Cousin Florence robbed the desk?"

"No, sir; I don't. Florence wouldn't do such a thing," said Dodger, warmly.

"Florence. Is that the way you speak of a young lady?"

"She tells me to call her Florence. I used to call her Miss Florence, but she didn't care for it."

"It seems you two have become very intimate," said Curtis, with a sneer.

"Florence is a good friend to me. I never had so good a friend before."

"All that is very affecting; however, it isn't to the point. Do you know," he continued, in a sterner tone, "that I could have you arrested for entering and breaking open my uncle's desk with burglarious intent?"

"I suppose you could," said Dodger; "but Florence would testify that I took nothing."

"Am I to understand, then, that you refuse to give me any information as to the will and the money?"

"No, sir; I don't refuse. I would tell you if I knew."

Curtis regarded the boy in some perplexity.

He had every appearance of telling the truth.

Dodger had one of those honest, truthful countenances which lend confirmation to any words spoken. If the boy told the truth, what could have become of the will - and the money? As to the former, it might be possible that his uncle had destroyed it, but the disappearance of the money presented an independent difficulty.

"The will is all I care for," he said, at length. "The thief is welcome to the money, though there was a considerable sum."

"I would find the will for you if I could," said Dodger, earnestly.

"You are positive you didn't give it to Bolton?"

"Positive, sir. I haven't seen Tim since that night."

"You may be speaking the truth, or you may not. I will talk with you again to-morrow," and Curtis arose from his chair.

"You don't mean to keep me here?" said Dodger, in alarm.

"I shall be obliged to do so."

"I won't stay!" exclaimed Dodger, in excitement, and he ran to the door, meaning to get out; but Curtis drew a pistol from his pocket and aimed it at the boy.

"Understand me, boy," he said, "I am in earnest, and I am not to be trifled with."

Dodger drew back, and Curtis opened the door and went out, bolting it after him.

CHAPTER XIX

AN ATTEMPT TO ESCAPE

While Dodger had no discomfort to complain of, it occurred to him that Florence would be alarmed by his long absence, for now it seemed certain that he would have to remain overnight.

If only he could escape he would take care not to fall into such a trap again.

He went to the window and looked out, but the distance to the ground was so great - for the room was on the third floor - that he did not dare to imperil his life by attempting a descent.

If there had been a rope at hand he would not have felt afraid to make the attempt.

He examined the bed to see if it rested upon cords, but there were slats instead.

As has already been said, there were no houses near by.

That part of the city had not been much settled, and it was as solitary as it is in the outskirts of a country village.

If he could only reveal his position to some person outside, so as to insure interference, he might yet obtain his freedom.

With this thought he tore a blank leaf from one of the books in the room, and hastily penciled the following lines:

> "I am kept a prisoner in this house. I was induced to come here by a trick. Please get some one to join you, and come and demand my release."

Some weeks before Dodger could not have written so creditable a note, but he had greatly improved since he had been under the influence and instruction of Florence.

Dodger now posted himself at the window and waited anxiously for some one to pass, so that he might attract his attention and throw down the paper.

He had to wait for fifteen minutes. Then he saw approaching a young man, not far from twenty-one, who looked like a young mechanic, returning from his daily work.

Now was Dodger's opportunity. He put his head out of the window and called out:

"Hello, there!"

The young man looked and saw him at the window.

"What do you want?" he asked.

"Catch this paper, and read what there is on it." He

threw down the leaf, which, after fluttering in the gentle evening breeze, found its way to the ground and was picked up.

After reading it, the young man looked up and said: "I'll go around to the door and inquire."

He was as good as his word. He went to the outer door and rang the bell.

Julius came to the door.

"What's wanted, boss?" he said.

"You've got a boy locked up in a room."

"Who told you, boss?"

"He threw down a paper to me, telling me he was kept a prisoner."

"What did he say?" asked Julius.

The young man read the note aloud.

"What have to say to that, you black imp?" he demanded, sternly.

The ready wit of Julius served him in this emergency.

"Dat boy is crazy as a loon, boss!" he answered, readily. "We have to keep him shut up for fear he'll kill some of us."

"You don't say!" ejaculated the young mechanic. "He don't look like it."

"No, he don't; dat's a fact, boss. Fact is, dat boy is the artfullest lunytick you ever seed. He tried to kill his mother last week."

"Is that true?"

"Dat's so, boss. And all de while he looks as innocent as a baby. If I was to let him out he'd kill somebody, sure."

"I never would have believed it," said the young man.

"If you want to take the risk, boss, you might go up and see him. I believe he's got a carvin'-knife about him, but I don't dare to go up and get it away. It would be as much as this niggah's life is worth."

"No," answered the young man, hastily. "I don't want to see him. I never did like crazy folks. I'm sorry I gave you the trouble to come to the door."

"Oh, no trouble, boss."

"I guess I've fixed dat boy!" chuckled Julius. "Ho, ho! he can't get ahead of old Julius! Crazy as a loon, ho, ho!"

Dodger waited anxiously for the young man to get through his interview. He hoped that he would force his way up to the third floor, draw the bolt, and release him from his imprisonment.

He kept watch at the window, and when the young man reappeared, he looked at him eagerly. "Did you ask them to let me out?" he shouted. The other looked up at him with an odd expression of suspicion and repulsion.

"You're better off where you are," he said, rather impatiently.

"But they have locked me up here."

"And reason enough, too!"

"What makes you say that?"

"Because you're crazy as a loon."

"Did the black man say that?" inquired Dodger, indignantly.

"Yes, he did - said you tried to kill your mother, and had a carving-knife hidden in the room."

"It's a lie - an outrageous lie!" exclaimed Dodger, his eyes flashing.

"Don't go into one of your tantrums," said the man, rather alarmed; "it won't do any good."

"But I want you to understand that I am no more crazy than you are."

"Sho? I know better. Where's your carving-knife?"

"I haven't got any; I never had any. That negro has been telling you lies. Just go to the door again, and insist on seeing me."

"I wouldn't dast to. You'd stab me," said the man, fearfully.

"Listen to me!" said Dodger, getting out of patience. "I'm not crazy. I'm a newsboy and baggage-smasher. An old man got me to bring his valise here, and then locked me up. Won't you go around to the station-house and send a policeman here?"

"I'll see about it," said the young man, who did not believe a word that Dodger had said to him.

"He won't do it!" said Dodger to himself, in a tone of discouragement. "That miserable nigger has made him believe I am a lunatic. I'll have him up, anyway."

Forthwith he began to pound and kick so forcibly, that Julius came upstairs on a run, half inclined to believe that Dodger had really become insane.

"What do you want, boy?" he inquired from outside the door.

"I want you to unbolt the door and let me out."

"I couldn't do it, nohow," said Julius. "It would be as much as my place is worth."

"I will give you a dollar - five dollars - if you will only let me out. The man who brought me here is a bad man, who is trying to cheat his cousin - a young lady - out of a fortune."

"Don't know nothin' 'bout that," said Julius.

"He has no right to keep me here."

"Don't know nothin' 'bout that, either. I'm actin' accordin' to orders."

"Look here," said Dodger, bethinking himself of what had just happened. "Did you tell that young man who called here just now that I was crazy?"

Julius burst into a loud guffaw.

"I expect I did," he laughed. "Said you'd got a long carvin'-knife hid in de room."

"What made you lie so?" demanded Dodger, sternly.

"Couldn't get rid of him no other way. Oh, how scared he looked when I told him you tried to kill your mother."

And the negro burst into another hearty laugh which exasperated Dodger exceedingly.

"How long is Mr. Waring going to keep me here? Did he tell you?" Dodger asked, after a pause.

"No; he didn't say."

"When is he coming here again?"

"Said he'd come to-morrow most likely."

"Will you bring me a light?"

"Couldn't do it. You'd set the house on fire."

It seemed useless to prolong the conversation.

Dodger threw himself on the bed at an early hour, but he did not undress, thinking there might possibly be a chance to escape during the night.

But the morning came and found him still a prisoner, but not in the solitary dwelling.

CHAPTER XX

A MIDNIGHT RIDE

Curtis Waring had entrapped Dodger for a double purpose.

It was not merely that he thought it possible the boy had the will, or knew where it was. He had begun to think of the boy's presence in New York as dangerous to his plans.

John Linden might at any time learn that the son, for whose appearance he had grieved so bitterly, was still living in the person of this street boy. Then there would be an end of his hopes of inheriting the estate.

Only a few months more and the danger would be over, for he felt convinced that his uncle's tenure of life would be brief. The one essential thing, then, seemed to be to get Dodger out of the city.

The first step had already been taken; what the next was will soon appear.

Scarcely had Dodger failed in his attempt to obtain outside assistance when an unaccountable drowsiness overcame him, considerably to his surprise.

"I don't know what's come to me," he said to himself. "It can't be more than seven or eight o'clock, and yet I feel so sleepy I can hardly keep my eyes open. I haven't worked any harder than usual to-day, and I can't understand it."

Dodger had reason to be surprised, for he didn't usually retire till eleven o'clock.

In a city like New York, where many of the streets are tolerably well filled even at midnight, people get in the way of sitting up much later than in the country, and Dodger was no exception to this rule.

Yet here he was ready to drop off to sleep before eight o'clock. To him it was a mystery, for he did not know that the cup of tea which he had drunk at supper had been drugged by direction of Curtis Waring, with an ulterior purpose, which will soon appear.

"I may as well lie down, as there is nothing else to do," thought Dodger. "There isn't much fun sitting in the dark. If I can sleep, so much the better."

Five minutes had scarcely passed after his head struck the pillow, when our hero was fast asleep.

At eleven o'clock a hack stopped in front of the house, and Curtis Waring descended from it.

"Stay here," he said to the driver. "There will be another passenger. If you are detained I will make it right when I come to pay you."

"All right, sir," said the hackman. "I don't care how long it is if I am paid for my time."

Curtis opened the door with a pass-key, and found Julius dozing in a chair in the hall.

"Wake up, you sleepy-head," he said. "Has anything happened since I left here?"

"Yes, sir; the boy tried to get away."

"Did he? I don't see how he could do that. You kept the door bolted, didn't you?"

"Yes, sir; but he throwed a piece of paper out'n de window, sayin' he was kep' a prisoner here. A young man picked it up, and came to de house to ax about it."

Curtis looked alarmed.

"What did you say?" he inquired, apprehensively.

"Told him de boy was crazy as a loon - dat he tried to kill his mother las' week, and had a carvin'-knife hid in his room."

"Good, Julius! I didn't give you credit for such a fertile imagination.

"What's dat, massa?" asked Julius, looking puzzled.

"I didn't know you were such a skillful liar."

"Yah! yah!" laughed Julius, quite comprehending this compliment. "I reckon I can twis' de trufe pretty well, Massa Curtis!"

"You have done well, Julius," said Curtis, approvingly. "Here's a dollar!"

The negro was quite effusive in his gratitude.

"What did the young man say?"

"He looked scared. I tol' him he could go up and see de boy if he wasn't afeared of the carvin'-knife, but he said he guessed he wouldn't - he didn't like crazy folks."

Curtis laughed heartily.

"So it all ended as it should. Did the boy make any more trouble?"

"Yes; he pounded and kicked till I had to go up and see what was the matter. I didn't give him no satisfaction, and I guess he went to bed."

"He ought to be in a deep sleep by this time. I will go up and see. Go up with me, Julius, for I may have to ask you to help me bring him down."

Though Julius was naturally a coward, he felt quite brave when he had company, and he at once went upstairs with Curtis Waring.

Curtis drew the bolt, and, entering the chamber, his glance fell upon Dodger, fast asleep on the bed.

"I am glad the boy did not undress," he said. "It will save me a great deal of trouble. Now, Julius, you can take his feet and I will lift his head, and we will take him downstairs."

"S'pos'n he wakes up, Massa Curtis?"

"He won't wake up. I took care the sleeping potion should be strong enough to produce profound slumber for eighteen hours."

"Seems as if he was dead," said Julius, nervously.

"Tush, you fool! He's no more dead than you or I."

The hackman looked curious when the two men appeared with their sleeping burden, and Curtis felt that some explanation was required.

"The boy has a very painful disease," he said, "and the doctor gave him a sleeping draught. He is going abroad for his health, and, under the circumstances, I think it best not to wake him up. Drive slowly and carefully to Pier No. -, as I don't want the boy aroused if it can be helped."

"All right, sir."

"Julius, you may lock the door and come with me. I shall need your help to get him on board the ship."

"All right, Massa Curtis."

"And, mind you, don't go to sleep in the carriage, you black rascal!" added Curtis, as he saw that the negro found it hard to keep his eyes open.

"All right, massa, I'll keep awake. How am I to get home?"

"I will instruct the hackman to take you home."

"Yah, yah; I'll be ridin' like a gentleman!"

The journey was successfully accomplished, but it took an hour, for, according to directions, the hackman did not force his pace, but drove slowly, till he reached the North River pier indicated.

At the pier was a large, stanch vessel - the *Columbia* - bound for San Francisco, around Cape Horn.

All was dark, but the second officer was pacing the deck.

Curtis Waring hailed him.

"What time do you get off?"

"Early to-morrow morning."

"So the captain told me. I have brought you a passenger."

"The captain told me about him."

"Is his stateroom ready?"

"Yes, sir. You are rather late."

"True; and the boy is asleep, as you will see. He is going to make the voyage for his health, and, as he has been suffering some pain, I thought I would not wake him up. Who will direct me to his stateroom?"

The mate summoned the steward, and Dodger, still unconscious, was brought on board and quietly transferred to the bunk that had been prepared for him.

It was a critical moment for poor Dodger, but he was

quite unconscious of it.

"What is the boy's name?" asked the mate.

"Arthur Grant. The captain has it on his list. Is he on board?"

"Yes; but he is asleep."

"I do not need to see him. I have transacted all necessary business with him - and paid the passage money. Julius, bring the valise."

Julius did so.

"This contains the boy's clothing. Take it to the stateroom, Julius."

"All right, Massa Curtis."

"What is your usual time between New York and San Francisco?" asked Curtis, addressing the mate.

"From four to six months. Four months is very short, six months very long. We ought to get there in five months, or perhaps a little sooner, with average weather."

"Very well. I believe there is no more to be said. Good-night!"

"Good-night, sir."

"So he is well out of the way for five months!" soliloquized Curtis. "In five months much may happen. Before that time I hope to be in possession of my uncle's property. Then I can snap my fingers at fate."

CHAPTER XXI

A SEASICK PASSENGER

The good ship *Columbia* had got fifty miles under way before Dodger opened his eyes.

He looked about him languidly at first, but this feeling was succeeded by the wildest amazement, as his eyes took in his unusual surroundings.

He had gone to sleep on a bed - he found himself on awakening in a ship's bunk.

He half arose in his birth, but the motion of the vessel and a slight feeling of dizziness compelled him to resume a recumbent position.

"I must be dreaming," thought Dodger. "It's very queer. I am dreaming I am at sea. I suppose that explains it."

He listened and heard the swish of the waters as they beat against the sides of the vessel.

He noted the pitching of the ship, and there was an unsteady feeling in his head, such as those who have gone to sea will readily recall.

Dodger became more and more bewildered.

"If it's a dream, it's the most real dream I ever had," he said to himself.

"This seems like a ship's cabin," he continued, looking about him. "I think if I got up I should be seasick. I wonder if people ever get seasick in dreams?"

There was another pitch, and Dodger instinctively clung to the edge of his berth, to save himself from being thrown out.

"Let me see," he said, trying to collect his scattered recollection. "I went to sleep in a house uptown - a house to which Curtis Waring lured me, and then made me a prisoner. The house was somewhere near One Hundred and Twenty-fifth Street. Now it seems as if I was on board a ship. How could I get here? I wish somebody would come in that I could ask."

As no one came in, Dodger got out of the berth, and tried to stand on the cabin floor.

But before he knew it he was staggering like one intoxicated, and his head began to feel bad, partly, no doubt, on account of the sleeping potion which he had unconsciously taken.

At this moment the steward entered the cabin. "Hello, young man! Have you got up?" he asked.

"Where am I?" asked Dodger, looking at him with a dazed expression.

"Where are you? You're on the good ship *Columbia*,

to be sure?"

"Are we out to sea?"

"Of course you are."

"How far from land?"

"Well, about fifty miles, more or less, I should judge."

"How long have I been here?"

"It seems to me you have a poor memory. You came on board last evening."

"I suppose Curtis Waring brought me," said Dodger, beginning to get his bearings.

"There was a gentleman came with you - so the mate told me. I don't know his name."

"Where is the ship bound?"

"To San Francisco, around Cape Horn. I supposed you knew that."

"I never heard of the ship *Columbia* before, and I never had any idea of making a sea voyage."

The steward looked surprised.

"I suppose your guardian arranged about that. Didn't he tell you?"

"I have no guardian."

"Well, you'll have to ask Capt. Barnes about that. I know nothing, except that you are a passenger, and that your fare has been paid."

"My fare paid to San Francisco?" asked Dodger, more and more at sea, both mentally and physically.

"Yes; we don't take any deadheads on the *Columbia*."

"Can you tell me what time it is?"

"About twelve o'clock. Do you feel hungry?"

"N - not very," returned Dodger, as a ghastly expression came over his face, and he tumbled back into his berth, looking very pale.

The steward smiled.

"I see how it is," he said; "you are getting initiated."

"What's that?" muttered Dodger, feebly.

"You're going to be seasick. You'll hardly be able to appear at the dinner table."

"It makes me sick to think of eating," said Dodger, feebly.

As he sank back into his berth, all thoughts of his unexpected position gave way to an overpowering feeling of seasickness.

He had never been tried in this way before, and he found the sensation far from agreeable.

"If only the vessel would stop pitching," he groaned. "Oh, how happy I should be if I were on dry land."

But the vessel wouldn't stop - even for a minute.

The motion, on the other hand, seemed to increase, as was natural, for they were getting farther and farther from land and were exposed to the more violent winds that swept the open ocean.

There is something about seasickness that swallows up and draws away all minor cares and anxieties, and Dodger was too much affected to consider how or why it was that he so unexpectedly found himself a passenger to California.

"Lie flat on your back," said the steward. "You will feel better if you do."

"How long is it going to last?" groaned Dodger, feeling quite miserable.

"Oh, you'll feel better to-morrow. I'll bring you some porridge presently. You can get that down, and it is better to have something on your stomach."

He was right. The next day Dodger felt considerably better, and ventured to go upon deck. He looked about him in surprise.

There had been a storm, and the waves were white with foam.

As far as the eye could see there was a tumult and an uproar.

The ship was tossed about like a cockle shell. But the sailors went about their work unruffled. It was no new sight for them.

Though his head did not feel exactly right, the strong wind entered Dodger's lungs, and he felt exhilarated. His eyes brightened, and he began to share in the excitement of the scene.

Pacing the deck was a stout, bronzed seaman, whose dress made it clear even to the inexperienced eyes of Dodger that he was the captain.

"Good-morning, Master Grant," he said, pleasantly. "Are you getting your sea legs on?"

The name was unfamiliar to Dodger, but he could see that the remark was addressed to him.

"Yes, sir," he answered.

"Ever been to sea before?"

"No, sir."

"You'll get used to it. Bless me, you'll stand it like an old sailor before we get to 'Frisco."

"Is it a long voyage, captain?" asked Dodger.

"Five months, probably. We may get there a little sooner. It depends on the winds and weather."

"Five months," said Dodger to himself, in a tone of dismay.

The captain laughed.

"It'll be a grand experience for a lad like you, Arthur!" said the captain, encouragingly.

Arthur! So his name was Arthur! He had just been called Master Grant, so Arthur Grant was his name on board ship.

Dodger was rather glad to have a name provided, for he had only been known as Dodger heretofore, and this name would excite surprise. He had recently felt the need of a name, and didn't see why this wouldn't answer his purpose as well as any other.

"I must write it down so as not to forget it," he resolved. "It would seem queer if I forgot my own name."

"I shouldn't enjoy it much if I were going to be seasick all the time," he answered.

"Oh, a strong, healthy boy like you will soon be all right. You don't look like an invalid."

"I never was sick in my life."

"But your guardian told me he was sending you on a sea voyage for your health."

"Did Mr. Waring say that?"

"Yes; didn't you know the object of your sea trip?" asked Capt. Barnes, in surprise.

"No."

"There may be some tendency to disease in your system - some hereditary tendency," said the captain, after a pause.

"Were your parents healthy?"

"They - died young," answered Dodger, hesitatingly.

"That accounts for your guardian's anxiety. However, you look strong enough, in all conscience; and if you're not healthy, you will be before the voyage ends."

"I don't know what I am to do for clothes," said Dodger, as a new source of perplexity presented itself. "I can't get along with one shirt and collar for five months."

"You will find plenty of clothes in your valise. Hasn't it been given you?"

"No, sir."

"You may ask the steward for it. You didn't think your guardian would send you on a five-months' voyage without a change of clothing, did you?"

And the captain laughed heartily.

"I don't know Mr. Waring very well," said Dodger, awkwardly.

As he went downstairs to inquire about his valise, this question haunted him:

"Why did Curtis Waring send him on a sea voyage?"

CHAPTER XXII

THE OTHER PASSENGER

Dodger sought the steward, and asked for his valise.

"Isn't it in your stateroom?" asked that functionary.

"I haven't seen it."

"I remember now. It was put with the luggage of the other passenger. I will show it to you."

He took Dodger to a part of the ship where freight was stored, and pointed to a sizable valise with a card attached to it on which was inscribed the name: "Arthur Grant."

"This must be yours," he said.

"Yes, I suppose so," answered Dodger, glad to have found out the new name which had been given him, otherwise he would have supposed the valise belonged to some other person.

He took the valise to his stateroom, and, finding a key tied to the handles, he opened it at once.

It proved to contain a very fair supply of

underclothing, socks, handkerchiefs, etc., with a tooth brush, a hair brush and comb, and a sponge. Never in his life had Dodger been so well supplied with clothing before. There were four white shirts, two tennis shirts, half a dozen handkerchiefs and the same number of socks, with three changes of underclothing.

"I begin to feel like a gentleman," said Dodger to himself, complacently.

That was not all. At the bottom of the valise was an envelope, sealed, on which was inscribed the name: "Dodger."

"That is for me, at any rate," thought our hero. "I suppose it is from Curtis Waring."

He opened the envelope, and found inclosed twenty-five dollars in bills, with a few lines written on a half-sheet of paper. These Dodger read, with interest and curiosity. They were as follows:

> "Dodger: - The money inclosed is for you. When you reach California you will find it of use. I have sent you out there because you will find in a new country a better chance to rise than in the city of New York. I advise you to stay there and grow up with the country. In New York you were under the influence of a bad man, from whom it is best that you should be permanently separated. I know something of the early history of Tim Bolton. He was detected in a crime, and fled to escape the consequences. You are not his son, but his nephew. Your mother was his sister, but quite superior to himself. Your right name is Arthur Grant, and it will be well for you to assume it hereafter. I have

entered you in the list of passengers under that name.

"I thought you had taken the will from my uncle's desk, but I am inclined to think you had nothing to do with it. If you know where it is, or whether Bolton has it, I expect you to notify me in return for the money I have expended in your behalf. In that case you can write to me, No. - Madison Avenue.

"Curtis Waring."

Dodger read the letter over twice, and it puzzled him.

"He seems from the letter to take an interest in me," he soliloquized. "At any rate, he has given me money and clothes, and paid my passage to California. What for, I wonder? I don't believe it is to get me away from the bad influence of Tim. There must be some other reason."

There was another part of the letter with which Dodger did not agree.

Curtis asserted positively that he was the nephew of Tim Bolton, while he was positive that there was no relationship between them.

In that case Curtis must have been an early acquaintance of Tim's. At any rate, he seemed to know about his past life.

Dodger now comprehended his present situation fully. He was a passenger on the ship *Columbia*, and there was no chance of leaving it. He had ascertainel on inquiry that the vessel would not put in anywhere, but would make the long voyage direct. It would be over four months, at any rate, before he could communicate with Florence, and in the meantime, she and Mrs. O'Keefe, whom he recognized as a good friend, would conclude that he was dead.

It was very provoking to think that he could not even telegraph, as that would relieve all anxiety, and he felt sure that Florence was enough his friend to feel anxious about him.

He had just closed up his valise, when a young man of dark complexion and of an attractive, intellectual expression, entered the cabin.

He nodded pleasantly to Dodger, and said:

"I suppose this is Arthur Grant?"

"Yes, sir," answered Dodger, for he had decided to adopt the name.

"We ought to become close friends, for we are, I believe, the only passengers."

"Then you are a passenger, too?" said Dodger, deciding, after a brief scrutiny, that he should like his new acquaintance.

"Yes. My name is Randolph Leslie. I have been, for the last five years, a reporter on leading New York daily papers, and worked so closely that my health has become somewhat affected. My doctor recommended a sea voyage, and I have arranged for a pretty long one."

"What papers have you worked for?"

"Oh, all the leading ones - *Tribune, World, Herald,* and *Sun* - sometimes one, and sometimes another. Your reason for taking this trip can hardly be the same as mine. You don't look as if your health required you to travel."

"No," answered Dodger, smiling; "but I understand that the gentleman who engaged my passage said I was going to sea for my health."

"If I were as robust as you, I shouldn't give much thought to my health. Do you intend to remain in California?"

"I don't know what I do intend," replied Dodger. "I didn't know I was going to California at all until I woke up in my stateroom."

The young man looked surprised.

"Didn't you know the destination of the vessel when you came on board?" he asked.

"I was brought aboard in my sleep."

"This is curious. It looks to me as if you had a story to tell.

"Of course, I don't want to be curious, but if there is anyway in which I can help you, by advice, or in any other way, I am quite ready to do so."

Dodger paused, but only briefly. This young man looked friendly, and might help him to penetrate the mystery which at present baffled him.

At any rate, his experience qualified him to give friendly advice, and of this Dodger felt that he stood in need.

"I ought to tell you, to begin with," he said, "that I am a poor boy, and made my living as best I could, by carrying baggage, selling papers, etc."

"I don't think any the worse of you for that. Did you live at the lodging houses?"

"No; until lately I lived with a man who keeps a saloon on the Bowery, and tended bar for him."

"What was his name? As a reporter I know the Bowery pretty well."

"Tim Bolton."

"Tim Bolton? I know his place well. I think I must have seen you there. Your face looked familiar to me as soon as I set eyes on you."

"Very likely. A good many people came into Tim's. I couldn't pretend to remember them all."

"Was Tim a relative of yours?"

"I don't believe he was. I always thought that he got hold of me when I was a kid. I don't remember the time when I wasn't with him."

"I suppose you have always lived in New York?"

"No; I lived for several years in Australia. Tim was in the same business there. I came on with him a year or more since."

"Do you think you ever lived in New York before?"

"Yes; Tim has told me that I was born in New York."

"I understand that you have left Tim now?"

"Yes."

"Why, may I ask?"

"Because I didn't like the business he was in. But I liked it better than the one he wanted me to go into."

"What was that?"

"Burglary."

The young reporter started in surprise.

"Well," he said, "this is a new tack for Tim. However, I never looked upon him as a man who would shrink from any violation of the laws, except murder. I don't think he would do that."

"No; Tim isn't quite so bad. He isn't the worst man alive, though he is a rather hard customer. It was his wanting me to enter a house on Madison Avenue and open a desk that led to me going on this trip."

"Tell me about it, if you don't mind."

Thus invited, Dodger told his story to Randolph Leslie, keeping nothing back.

He finished by showing him the letter he had found in the valise.

CHAPTER XXIII

THROUGH THE GOLDEN GATE

"Well, this is certainly a remarkable letter," said the reporter, as he handed it back to Dodger. "I am at a loss to understand the interest which this man appears to feel in you."

"I look upon him as my enemy," said Dodger. "But an enemy doesn't spend so much money upon another as he has."

"Unless he has object in it," amended Leslie, shrewdly. "Do you know of any connection this man has with you?"

"No; I never heard of him until I entered his house," and Dodger flushed as he thought that his entrance into the mansion on Madison Avenue had been as a burglar.

"It seems to me that he knows more about you than you do about him. It also seems to me that he is anxious to get you out of New York, the farther the better."

"But what harm could I do him in New York?" asked Dodger, puzzled.

"That is the question which I cannot answer. You say he was instrumental in getting his Cousin Florence out of the house?"

"Yes; he wanted to marry her."

"And she would not consent?"

"No; I think she hates him."

"How old is she?"

"Seventeen."

"And he?"

"He looks about thirty-five."

"The difference in years isn't great enough to constitute an obstacle, provided she loved him. I am thirty years old."

"I am sure Florence would prefer you to Curtis Waring."

"Don't flatter me. I am vain enough already. The time may come when I may ask your good offices with Miss Linden. What I was about to ask was: Is Miss Linden also entitled to a share in her uncle's estate?"

"She is just as nearly related to him as Mr. Waring."

"Then I can understand his wishing to get rid of her. I don't know why he should want to send you to a distance. I suppose there can't be any relationship?"

"Is it likely that I - a poor street boy - should be related to a rich man like Mr. Linden?"

"It doesn't seem likely, I admit," said Leslie, musingly. "Well, I suppose," he continued, after a pause, "there is no use in speculating about the matter now. The important point is, what are we to do with ourselves during the four or five months we must spend on shipboard?"

"I don't know what I can do," said Dodger. "I can't sell papers, and I can't smash baggage."

"And there appears to be no need of your doing either, as you are provided with board and lodging till we reach shore."

"That seems strange to me, for I've always had to hustle for a living."

"I was about to make a proposal to you. But first let me ask you about your education. I suppose you are not an accomplished scholar?"

"I'm about as ignorant as they make 'em," answered Dodger, drolly. "Tim was afraid to send me to college, for fear I'd get to know too much for my business."

"Tending bar does not require an acquaintance with Latin and Greek. Would you like to know more?"

"I wish I did. Florence was teaching me nights when I was in New York. Now I've got to give up all that."

"Not necessarily. Listen to me, Arthur. Before I came to New York to go into journalism, I taught school for two years; and I believe I may say that I was tolerably successful. Suppose I take you as a scholar?"

"I should like it very much, Mr. Leslie, but I'm afraid I haven't got money enough to pay you."

"That is true. You will need all the money you have when you land in California. Twenty-five dollars won't go far - still you have all the money that is necessary, for I do not intend to charge you anything."

"You are very kind to me, Mr. Leslie, considerin' you don't know me," said Dodger, gratefully.

"On the contrary, I think I know you very well. But about the kindness - my motives are somewhat mixed. I should like to do you a service, but I should also like to find employment for myself that will make the days less monotonous. I have a collection of books in my trunk, enough for our needs, and if you will agree we will commence our studies to-morrow."

"I should like it very much. I'd like to show Florence, when I see her, that I have improved. Till I saw her I didn't care much, but when I talk with her I feel awfully ignorant."

"In four months a great deal can be accomplished. I don't know how quick you are to learn. After we have had one or two lessons I can judge better."

Two days later Mr. Leslie pronounced his opinion, and a favorable one.

"You have not exaggerated your ignorance," he said to Dodger. "You have a great deal to learn, but on the other hand you are quick, have a retentive memory, and are very anxious to learn. I shall make something of you."

"I learn faster with you than with Florence," said Dodger.

"Probably she would succeed better with girls, but I hold that a male teacher is better for boys. How long are you willing to study every day?"

"As long as you think best."

"Then we will say from two to three hours. I think you have talent for arithmetic. I don't expect to make you fit for a bookkeeper, but I hope to make you equal to most office boys by the time we reach San Francisco. What do you intend to do in California?"

"I don't know. I should like to go back to New York, but I shall not have money enough."

"No; twenty-five dollars would go but a little way toward the passage. Evidently Mr. Waring did not intend to have you return, or he would have provided you with more."

"That is just why I should like to go back. I am afraid he will do some harm to Florence."

"And you would like to be on hand to protect her?"

"Yes."

Randolph Leslie smiled.

"You seem to take a great deal of interest in Florence, if I may make as free with her name as you do."

"Yes; I do, Mr. Leslie."

"If you were only a little older I might suspect the nature of that interest."

"I am older than she is."

"In years, yes. But a young lady of seventeen, brought up as she has been, is older by years than a boy of eighteen. I don't think you need apprehend any harm to Miss Linden, except that Mr. Waring may cheat her out of her rightful share of the inheritance. Is her uncle in good health?"

"No, sir; he is a very feeble man."

"Is he an old man?"

"Not so very old. I don't believe he is over sixty."

Really Mr. Linden was but fifty-four, but, being a confirmed invalid, he looked older.

"Should you say that he was likely to live very long?"

"No," answered Dodger. "He looks as if you could knock him over with a feather. Besides, I've heard Florence say that she was afraid her uncle could not live long."

"Probably Curtis Waring is counting upon this. If he can keep Florence and her uncle apart for a few months, Mr. Linden will die, and he will inherit the whole estate. What is this will he speaks of in the letter you showed me?"

"I don't know, sir."

"Whatever the provisions are, it is evident that he thinks it important to get it into his possession. If favorable to him, he will keep it carefully. If unfavorable, I think a man like him would not hesitate to suppress it."

"No doubt you are right, sir. I don't know much about wills," said Dodger.

"No; I suppose not. You never made any, I suppose," remarked the reporter, with a smile.

"I never had nothing to leave," said Dodger.

"Anything would be a better expression. As your tutor I feel it incumbent upon me to correct your grammar."

"I wish you would, Mr. Leslie. What do you mean to do when you get to San Francisco?"

"I shall seek employment on one of the San Farncisco daily papers. Six months or a year so spent will restore my health, and enable me to live without drawing upon my moderate savings."

"I expect I shall have to work, too, to get money to take me back to New York."

And now we must ask the reader to imagine four months and one week passed.

There had been favorable weather on the whole, and the voyage was unusually short.

Dodger and the reporter stood on deck, and with eager interest watched the passage through the Golden Gate. A little later and the queen city of the Pacific came in sight, crowning the hill on which a part of the city is built, with the vast Palace Hotel a conspicuous object in the foreground.

CHAPTER XXIV

FLORENCE IN SUSPENSE

We must now return to New York to Dodger's old home.

When he did not return at the usual hour, neither Florence nor Mrs. O'Keefe was particularly disturbed.

It was thought that he had gone on some errand of unusual length, and would return an hour or two late.

Eight o'clock came, the hour at which the boy was accustomed to repair to Florence's room to study, and still he didn't make his appearance.

"Dodger's late this evening, Mrs. O'Keefe," said Florence, going up to the room of her landlady.

"Shure he is. It's likely he's gone to Brooklyn or up to Harlem, wid a bundle. He'll be comin' in soon."

"I hope he will be well paid for the errand, since it keeps him so long."

"I hope so, too, Florence, for he's a good boy, is Dodger. Did I tell you how he served the rapscallion that tried to stale my apples the other day?"

"No; I would like to hear it."

"A big, black-bearded man came along, and asked me for an apple.

"'You can have one for two pennies,' says I.

"'But I haven't got them,' says he.

"'Then you must go widout it,' says I.

"'We'll see about that,' says he.

"And what do you think? - the fellow picked out one of my biggest apples, and was walkin' away! That made me mad.

"'Come back, you thafe of the worruld!' says I.

"'Silence, you old hag!' says he.

"Actilly he called me an old hag! I wanted to go after him, but there was two hoodlums hangin' round, and I knew they'd carry off some of my apples, when, just as I was at my wits' end, Dodger came round the corner.

"'Dodger,' I screamed, 'go after that man! He's taken one of my apples, widout lave or license!'

"Upon that, Dodger, brave as a lion, walked up to the man, and, says he:

"'Give back that apple, or pay for it!'

"'What's that to you, you impudent young rascal?' says the man, raisin' the apple to his mouth. But he didn't get a chance to bite it, for Dodger, with a flip of his hand, knocked it on the sidewalk, and picked it up.

"Wasn't the man mad just?"

"'I'll smash you, boy,' he growled.

"'I'm a baggage-smasher myself,' says Dodger, 'and I can smash as well as you.'

"Wid that the man up with his fist and struck at Dodger, but he dodged the blow, and gave him one for himself wid his right. Just then up came a cop.

"'What's all this?' says he.

"'That man tried to run off wid one of my apples,' says I.

"'Come along,' says the cop. 'You're wanted at the station-house.'

"'It's a lie,' says the man. 'I paid the woman for the apple, and that young rascal knocked it out of my hand.'

"'I know the boy,' says the cop, 'and he ain't one of that kind. I'll let you go if you buy five apples from the lady, and pay for 'em.'

"The man made up an ugly face, but he didn't want to be locked up, and so he paid me a dime for five apples."

"Dodger is very brave," said Florence. "Sometimes I think he is too daring. He is liable to get into trouble."

"If he does he'll get himself out of it, never you fear. Dodger can take care of himself."

Nine o'clock came, and Florence became alarmed. She had not been aware how much she had depended upon the company of her faithful friend, humble as his station was.

Again she went into Mrs. O'Keefe's room. The apple-woman had been out to buy some groceries and had just returned.

"I am getting anxious about Dodger," said Florence. "It is nine o'clock."

"And what's nine o'clock for a boy like him? Shure he's used to bein' out at all hours of the night."

"I shall feel relieved when he comes home. What should I do without him?"

"Shure I'd miss him myself; but it isn't the first time he has been out late."

"Perhaps that terrible Tim Bolton has got hold of him," suggested Florence.

"Tim isn't so bad, Florence. He isn't fit company for the likes of you, but there's worse men nor Tim."

"Didn't he send out Dodger to commit a burglary?"

"And if he hadn't you'd never made Dodger's acquaintance."

"That's true; but it doesn't make burglary any more

excusable. Don't you really think Tim Bolton has got hold of him?"

"If he has, he won't keep him long, I'll make oath of that. He might keep him over night, but Dodger would come back in the morning."

Florence was somewhat cheered by Mrs. O'Keefe's refusal to believe that Dodger was in any serious trouble, but she could not wholly free herself from uneasiness. When eleven o'clock came she went to bed very unwillingly, and got very little rest during the night. Morning came, and still Dodger did not show up. As we know, he was fairly started on his long voyage, though he had not yet recovered consciousness.

Florence took a very light breakfast, and at the usual time went to Mrs. Leighton's to meet her pupil. When the study hour was over, she did not remain to lunch, but hurried back, stopping at Mrs. O'Keefe's apple-stand just as that lady was preparing to go home to prepare dinner.

"Have you seen anything of Dodger, Mrs. O'Keefe?" asked Florence, breathlessly.

"No, I haven't, Florence. I've had my eye out watchin' for him, and he hasn't showed up."

"Is there anything we can do?" asked Florence, anxiously.

"Well, we might go around and see Tim - and find out whether he's got hold of him."

"Let us go at once."

"Shure I didn't know you cared so much for the boy," said Mrs. O'Keefe, with a shrewd look at Florence's anxious face.

"Why shouldn't I care for him? He is my only friend."

"Is he now? And what's the matter wid Bridget O'Keefe?" asked the apple-woman.

"Excuse me, Mrs. O'Keefe. I know very well you are my friend, and a kind friend, too. I should not have forgotten you."

"It's all right, Florence. You're flustrated like, and that's why you forget me."

"I have so few friends that I can't spare one," continued Florence.

"That's so. Come along wid me, and we'll see what Tim has to tell us."

A short walk brought the two strangely assorted companions to the entrance of Tim Bolton's saloon. "I'm afraid to go in, Mrs. O'Keefe," said Florence.

"Come along wid me, my dear, I won't let anything harm you. You ain't used to such a place, but I've been here more than once to fill the growler. Be careful as you go down the steps, Florence."

Tim Bolton was standing behind the bar, and as he heard steps he looked carelessly toward the entrance, but when he saw Florence, his indifference vanished.

He came from behind the bar, and advanced to meet her.

"Miss Linden," he said.

Florence shrank back and clung to her companion's arm.

"Is there anything I can do for you? I am a rough man, but I'm not so bad as you may think."

"That's what I told her, Tim," said Mrs. O'Keefe. "I told Florence there was worse men than you."

"Thank you, Mrs. O'Keefe. Can I offer you a glass of whiskey?"

The apple-woman was about to accept, but she felt an alarmed tug at her arm, and saw that Florence would be placed in an embarrassing position if she accepted. So, by an exercise of self-denial - for Mrs. O'Keefe was by no means insensible to the attractions of whiskey, though she never drank to excess - she said:

"Thank you kindly, Mr. Bolton. I won't take any just now; but I'll remind you of your offer another day."

"Have it your own way, Mrs. O'Keefe. And now, what can I do for you and Miss Linden?"

"Oh, Mr. Bolton," broke in Florence, unable to bear the suspense longer, "where is Dodger?"

CHAPTER XXV

FINDING THE CLEW

Tim Bolton looked at Florence in undisguised astonishment.

"Dodger!" he repeated. "How should I know? I supposed that you had lured him away from me."

"He didn't like the business you were in. He preferred to make a living in some other way."

"Then why do you ask me where he is?"

"Because he did not come home last night. Shure he rooms at my house," put in Mrs. O'Keefe, "and he hasn't showed up since -"

"And you thought I might have got hold of him?" said Bolton, inquiringly.

"Then you are mistaken. I haven't seen the boy for weeks."

Tim Bolton spoke so straightforwardly that there was no chance to doubt his word.

"When he was living with you, Mr. Bolton," continued

Florence, "did he ever stay away like this?"

"No," answered Bolton. "Dodger was always very regular about comin' home."

"Then something must have happened to him," said Florence, anxiously.

"He might have got run in," suggested the apple-woman. "Some of them cops is mighty officious."

"Dodger would never do anything to deserve arrest," Florence said, quickly.

"Thrue for you, Florence, but some innersent parties are nabbed. I know of one young man who was standin' on a strate corner waitin' for the cars, when a cop came up and arristed him for disorderly conduct."

"But that is shameful!" said Florence, indignantly.

"Thrue for you, my dear. We might go round to the police headquarters and inquire if the boy's been run in."

"What do you think, Mr. Bolton?" asked Florence.

Tim Bolton seemed busy thinking. Finally he brought down his hand forcibly on the bar, and said: "I begin to see through it."

Florence did not speak, but she fixed an eager look of inquiry on the face of the saloon-keeper.

"I believe Curtis Waring is at the bottom of this," he said.

"My cousin!" exclaimed Florence, in astonishment.

"Yes, your cousin, Miss Linden."

"But what can he have against poor Dodger! Is it because the boy has taken my part and is a friend to me?"

"He wouldn't like him any better on account of hat; but he has another and a more powerful reason."

"Would you mind telling me what it is? I cannot conceive what it can be."

"At present," answered Bolton, cautiously, "I prefer to say nothing on the subject. I will only say the boy's disappearance interferes with my plans, and I will see if I can't find out what has become of him."

"If you only will, Mr. Bolton, I shall be so grateful. I am afraid I have misjudged you. I thought you were an enemy of Dodger's."

"Then you were mistaken. I have had the boy with me since he was a kid, and though I've been rough with him at times, maybe, I like him, and I may some time have a chance to show him that old Tim Bolton is one of his best friends."

"I will believe it now, Mr. Bolton," said Florence, impulsively, holding out her hand to the burly saloon-keeper.

He was surprised, but it was evident that he was pleased, also, and he took the little hand respectfully in his own ample palm, and pressed it in a friendly manner.

"There's one thing more I want you to believe, Miss Linden," he said, "and that is, that I am your friend, also."

"Thank you, Mr. Bolton. And now let us all work together to find Dodger."

"You can count on me, Miss Linden. If you'll tell me where you live I'll send or bring you any news I may hear."

"I live with Mrs. O'Keefe, my good friend, here."

"I haven't my kyard with me, Tim," said the apple-woman, "but I'll give you my strate and number. You know my place of business?"

"Yes."

"If you come to me there I'll let Florence know whatever you tell me. She is not always at home."

The two went away relieved in mind, for, helpless and bewildered as they were, they felt that Tim Bolton would make a valuable ally.

When they had gone Tim turned to Hooker and Briggs, who were lounging at a table, waiting for some generous customer to invite them to the bar.

"Boys," said Tim, "has either of you seen anything of Dodger lately?"

"No," answered the two in unison.

"Have you heard anything of him?"

"I heard that he was baggage-smashin' down by the steamboat landings," said Hooker.

"Go down there, both of you, and see if you can see or hear anything of him."

"All right, Tim."

And the two left the saloon and took a westerly route toward the North River piers.

Three hours later they returned.

"Have you heard anything?" asked Bolton. "Did you see Dodger?"

"No; we didn't see him."

"But you heard something?"

"Yes; we found a boy, a friend of his, that said the last he saw of Dodger was last evenin'."

"Where did he see him?"

"Ncar the pier of the Albany boats."

"What was he doin'?"

"Carryin' a valise for a man."

"What kind of a man? How did he look?"

"He had gray hair and gray whiskers."

Tim was puzzled by the description.

If, as he suspected, Curtis were concerned in the abduction, this man could not have been he.

"The man was a passenger by the Albany boat, I suppose?"

"No; that was what looked queer. Before the Albany boat came in the man was lyin' round with his valise, and the boy thought he was goin' off somewhere. But when the boat came in he just mixed in with the passengers, and came up to the entrance of the pier. Two boys asked to carry his valise, but he shook his head till Dodger came round, and he engaged him right off."

Tim Bolton nodded knowingly.

"It was a plan," he said. "The man wanted to get hold of Dodger. What puzzles me is, that you said he was an old man."

"His hair and beard were gray."

"And Curtis has no beard, and his hair is black."

"But the boy said he didn't look like an old man, except the hair. He walked off like a young man."

Tim Bolton's face lighted up with sudden intelligence.

"I'll bet a hat it was Curtis in disguise," he soliloquized.

"That's all we could find out, Mr. Bolton," said Briggs, with another longing look at the bar.

"It is enough! You have earned your whiskey. Walk up, gentlemen!"

Hooker and Briggs needed no second invitation.

"Will either of you take a note for me to Mrs. O'Keefe? For another drink, of course."

"I will, Tim," said Hooker, eagerly.

"No; take me, Mr. Bolton," entreated Briggs.

"You can both go," said Tim, generously. "Wait a minute, and I'll have it ready for you."

He found a half sheet of note paper, and scribbled on it this message:

> "Mrs. O'Keefe: - Tell Miss Linden that I have a clew. I am almost surtin her cozen has got away with Dodger. He won't hurt him, but he will get him out of the city. Wen I hear more I will right.
>
> "T. Bolton."

CHAPTER XXVI

BOLTON MAKES A DISCOVERY

"I see it all," Bolton said to himself, thoughtfully. "Curtis Waring is afraid of the boy - and of me. He's circumvented me neatly, and the game is his - so far my little plan is dished. I must find out for certain whether he's had anything to do with gettin' Dodger out of the way, and then, Tim Bolton, you must set your wits to work to spoil his little game."

Bolton succeeded in securing the services of a young man who had experience at tending bar, and about eight o'clock, after donning his best attire, he hailed a Fourth Avenue surface car and got aboard.

Getting out at the proper street, he made his way to Madison Avenue, and ascended the steps of John Linden's residence.

The door was opened by Jane, who eyed the visitor with no friendly glance.

"What do you want?" she asked, in a hostile tone.

"Is Mr. Waring at home?"

"I don't know."

"Is Miss Florence at home?"

"Do you know her?" she asked.

"Yes; I am a friend of hers."

Jane evidently thought that Florence must have made some queer friends.

"Have you seen her lately?" she asked eagerly.

"I saw her to-day."

"Is she well?"

"Yes; she is well, but she is in trouble."

"Is she - Does she need any money?"

"No; it isn't that. The boy Dodger has disappeared, and she is afraid something has happened to him."

"Oh, I am so sorry! He was a good friend of Miss Florence."

"I see you know him. I am trying to help him and her."

"But you asked for Mr. Waring?" said Jane, suspiciously.

"So I did. Shall I tell you why?"

"I wish you would."

"I think he has something to do with gettin' Dodger out of the way, and I'm goin' to try to find out."

"He won't tell you."

"You don't understand. I shall make him think I am on his side. Was he at home last night?"

"He went away at dinner time, and he didn't come home till after twelve. I ought to know, for he forgot his latchkey, and I had to get up and let him in. I won't do it again. I'll let him stay out first."

"I see; he was with Dodger, no doubt. Did you say he was in?"

"No, sir; but he will be in directly. Won't you step into the library?"

"Shall I meet the old gentleman there?" asked Bolton, in a tone of hesitation.

"No. He goes up to his chamber directly after dinner."

"How is he?"

"I think he's failing."

"I hope there is no immediate danger," said Bolton, anxiously.

"No; but he's worrying about Miss Florence. It's my belief that if she were at home, he'd live a good while."

"Doesn't he ask for her?"

"Mr. Curtis tells him she'll come round soon if he'll only be firm. I don't see, for my part, why Mr. Linden wants her to marry such a disagreeable man. There's plenty better husbands she could get. Come in, sir, and I'll tell him as soon as he comes in. Shall you see Miss Florence soon?"

"I think so."

"Then tell her not to give up. Things will come right some time."

"I'll tell her."

Bolton was ushered into the library, where, amid the fashionable furniture he looked quite out of place. He did not feel so, however, for he drew a cigar out of his pocket and, lighting it nonchalantly, leaned back in a luxurious armchair and began to smoke.

"Curtis Waring is well fixed - that's a fact!" he soliloquized. "I suppose he is the master here, for the old man isn't likely to interfere. Still he will like it better when his uncle is out of the way."

He had to wait but fifteen minutes in solitude, for at the end of that time Curtis Waring appeared.

He paused on the threshold, and frowned when he saw who it was that awaited him.

"Jane told me that a gentleman was waiting to see me," he said.

"Well, she was right."

"And you, I suppose, are the gentleman?" said Curtis, in a sneering tone.

"Yes; I am the gentleman," remarked Bolton, coolly.

"I am not in the habit of receiving visits from gentlemen of your class. However, I suppose you have an object in calling."

"It shall go hard with me if I don't pay you for your sneers some day," thought Bolton; but he remained outwardly unruffled.

"Well," he answered, "I can't say that I have any particular business to see you about. I saw your cousin recently."

"Florence?" asked Curtis, eagerly.

"Yes."

"What did she say? Did you speak with her?"

"Yes. She doesn't seem any more willin' to marry you."

Curtis Waring frowned.

"She is a foolish girl," he said. "She doesn't know her own mind."

"She looks to me like a gal that knows her own mind particularly well."

"Pshaw! what can you know about it?"

"Then you really expect to marry her some time, Mr. Waring?"

"Certainly I do."

"And to inherit your uncle's fortune?"

"Of course. Why not?"

"I was thinkin' of the boy."

"The boy is dead -"

"What!" exclaimed Bolton, jumping to his feet in irresistible excitement.

"Don't be a fool. Wait till I finish my sentence. He is dead so far as his prospects are concerned. Who is there that can identify him with the lost child of John Linden?"

"I can."

"Yes; if any one would believe you. However, it is for your interest to keep silent."

"That is just what I want to know. I suppose you can make it for my interest."

"Yes, and will - after I get the property. I don't believe in counting my chickens before they are hatched."

"Of course you know that the boy has left me?" said Bolton.

"Yes," answered Curtis, indifferently. "He is with my cousin, I believe."

"Yes; and through her I can learn where he is, and get hold of him if I desire."

A cynical smile played over the face of Curtis Waring.

"Do you propose to get him back?" he asked, shrugging his shoulders.

"I am right," thought Bolton, shrewdly. "From his manner it is easy to see that Curtis is quite at ease as regards Dodger. He knows where he is!"

"You asked me what business I came about, Mr. Waring," he said, after a pause.

"Yes."

"Of course I am devoted to your interests, but is it quite fair to make me wait till you come into your fortune before allowing me anything?"

"I think so."

"You don't seem to consider that I can bring the boy here and make him known to your uncle as the son he lost so long ago?"

"You are quite sure you can bring the boy here?" asked Curtis.

"Why not? I have only to go to Florence and ask her to send the boy to me."

"You are quite at liberty to do so if you like, Tim Bolton," said Curtis, with a mocking smile. "I am glad, at any rate, that you have shown me what is in your mind. You are very sharp, but you are not quite so sharp as I am."

"I don't understand you."

"Then I will be more explicit. It's out of your power to make use of the boy against me, because -"

"Well?"

"Because he is not in the city."

"Where is he, then?"

"Where you are not likely to find him."

"If you have killed him -" Bolton began, but Curtis interrupted him.

"The boy is safe - I will tell you that much," he said; "but for reasons which you can guess, I think it better that he should be out of New York. When the proper time comes, and all is safe, he may come back, but not in time to help you in your cunning plans, Mr. Tim Bolton."

"Then, I suppose," said Bolton, assuming an air of mortification and discomfiture, "it is no use for me to remain here any longer."

"You are quite right. I wish you a pleasant journey home. Give my love to Florence when you see her."

"That man is a fiend!" soliloquized Bolton, as he walked back, leisurely, to his place of business. "Let me get hold of Dodger and I will foil him yet!"

CHAPTER XXVII

DODGER STRIKES LUCK

When Dodger landed in San Francisco, in spite of the fact that he had made the journey against his will, he felt a natural exhilaration and pleasure in the new and striking circumstances and scenes in which he found himself placed.

It was in the year 1877, and the city was by no means what it is now. Yet it probably contained not far from two hundred thousand people, lively, earnest, enterprising. All seemed busy and hopeful, and Dodger caught the contagion.

As he walked with the reporter to a modest hotel, where the rates were a dollar and a half a day, not far from Montgomery Street, Randolph Leslie asked:

"How do you like San Francisco thus far, Arthur?"

It will be remembered that Dodger, feeling that the name by which he had hitherto been known was hardly likely to recommend him, adopted the one given him by Curtis Waring.

"I think I shall like it ever so much," answered Dodger. "Everybody seems to be wideawake."

"Do you think you will like it better than New York?"

"I think a poor boy will have more of a chance of making a living here. In New York I was too well known. If I got a place anywhere some one would recognize me as Tim Bolton's boy - accustomed to tend bar - or some gentleman would remember that he had bought papers of me. Here nobody knows me, and I can start fair."

"There is a great deal in what you say," returned Leslie. "What do you think of trying to do?"

"First of all I will write a letter to Florence, and tell her I am all right. How long does it take a letter to go from here to New York?"

"About seven days."

"And it took us over four months! That seems wonderful."

"Yes; there is a great difference between coming by sea around Cape Horn and speeding across the country on an express train."

"If I could only know how Florence is getting along," Dodger said, anxiously. "I suppose she thinks I am dead."

"You forget the letter you gave to the vessel we spoke off the coast of Brazil."

"Yes; but do you think it went straight?"

"The chances are in favor of it. However, your idea is a

good one. Write, by all means, and then we will discuss future plans."

"What are your plans, Mr. Leslie?"

"I shall try to secure a reporter's berth on one of the daily papers - the *Call* or *Chronicle*. I will wait a few days, however, as I have a few hundred dollars by me, and can afford to take a little time to look around."

"I wish I were as well provided; but I have less than twenty-five dollars."

"Don't worry about that, Arthur," said Randolph, laying his hand affectionately on the boy's shoulder. "I shall not allow you to want."

"Thank you, Mr. Leslie," said Dodger, gratefully. "It's something new to me to have a friend like you. But I don't want to be any expense to you. I am large enough and strong enough to earn my own living."

"True; and I feel sure you will have a chance in this enterprising city."

They bought copies of the day's papers, and Dodger looked eagerly over the advertising columns.

At length he saw an advertisement that read as follows:

> WANTED - A young man of 18 or 20 to assist in the office of a local express. Inquire at No. - St."

"Do you think I would answer for such a place?" he asked.

"I don't see why not. At any rate, 'nothing venture, nothing gain.' You may as well go around and inquire. And, by the way, as your suit is rather shabby, let me lend you one of mine. We are of nearly the same size."

"Thank you, Mr. Leslie."

"Fine feathers make fine birds, you know, and a neat dress always increases the chances of an applicant for employment, though, when it is carried too far, it is apt to excite suspicion. I remember a friend of mine advertised for a bookkeeper. Among the applicants was a young man wearing a sixty-dollar suit, a ruffled shirt, a handsome gold watch and a diamond pin. He was a man of taste, and he was strongly impressed with the young man's elegant appearance. So, largely upon the strength of these, he engaged him, and in less than six months discovered that he had been swindled to the extent of eight hundred dollars by his aesthetic bookkeeper."

"Then I will leave my diamond pin at home," said Dodger, smiling. "Suppose they ask me for recomm-endations?"

"I will go with you and indorse you. I happen to know one or two prominent gentlemen in San Francisco - among them the president of a bank - and I presume my indorsement will be sufficient."

Dodger went back to the hotel, put on a suit of Mr. Leslie's, got his boots blacked, and then, in company with the young reporter, went to the express office.

"I am afraid some one will have been engaged already," said the reporter; "but if not, your chances will be good."

They entered a good-sized office on a prominent street, and Dodger inquired for Mr. Tucker.

A small man of about forty, keen-eyed and alert, eyed him attentively.

"I am Mr. Tucker," he said.

"I saw your advertisement for an assistant, Mr. Tucker," said Dodger, modestly; "have you filled the place?"

"Let me see," said Tucker, reflectively, "you are the ninth young man who has applied - but the place is still open."

"Then I am afraid you won't want me, as you have rejected so many."

"I don't know. How long have you been in the city?"

"I only just arrived."

"Where from?"

"From New York."

"Have you any idea of going to the mines when you get money enough?"

"I think I would prefer to remain in the city."

"Good! How is your education?"

"I have never been to college," answered Dodger, with a smile.

"Good! I don't care for your college men. I am a practical man myself."

"I am a poor scholar, but Mr. Leslie tells me I write a fair hand."

"Let me see a specimen of your writing."

Now Dodger had taken special pains on the voyage to improve his penmanship, with excellent results.

So it happened that the specimen which he furnished had the good fortune to please Mr. Tucker.

"Good!" he said. "You will, a part of the time, be taking orders. Your handwriting is plain and will do. Never mind about Latin and Greek. You won't need it. Chinese would be more serviceable to you here. When can you go to work?"

"To-morrow morning. To-day, if necessary," answered Dodger, promptly.

Mr. Tucker seemed pleased with his answer.

"To-morrow morning let it be, then! Hours are from eight in the morning till six at night."

"Very well, sir."

"Your wages will be fifteen dollars a week. How will that suit you?"

Dodger wanted to indulge in a loud whoop of exultation, for fifteen dollars was beyond his wildest hopes; but he was too politic to express his delight. So he contented himself with saying:

"I shall be quite satisfied with that."

"Oh, by the way, I suppose I ought to have some reference," said Mr. Tucker, "though as a general thing I judge a good deal by outward appearance."

"I can refer you to my friend, Mr. Leslie, here."

"And who will indorse him?" asked the expressman, shrewdly.

Leslie smiled.

"I see, Mr. Tucker, you are a thorough man of business. I can refer you to Mr. -, president of the - Bank in this city."

"That is sufficient, sir. I am sure you would not refer me to him unless you felt satisfied that he would speak favorably of you. I won't, therefore, take the trouble to inquire. Where are you staying?"

"At the Pacific Hotel; but we shall take a private apartment within a day or two."

As they passed out of the office, Randolph Leslie said:

"You've done splendidly, Arthur."

"Haven't I? I feel like a millionaire."

"As you are to go to work to-morrow, we may as well take up a room at once. It will be cheaper."

In a short time they had engaged a neat suite of rooms, two in number, not far from the Palace Hotel, at twenty dollars per month.

The next day Leslie procured a position on the San Francisco *Chronicle*, at twenty-five dollars per week.

CHAPTER XXVIII

FLORENCE RECEIVES A LETTER

The discovery, through Tim Bolton, that Curtis Waring had a hand in the disappearance of Dodger, partially relieved the anxiety of Florence - but only partially.

He might be detained in captivity, but even that was far better than an accident to life or limb.

She knew that he would try to get word to her at the earliest opportunity, in order to relieve her fears.

But week after week passed, and no tidings came.

At length, at the end of ten weeks, a note came to her, written on a rough sheet of paper, the envelope marked by a foreign stamp.

It ran thus:

"Dear Florence: - I am sure you have worried over my disappearance. Perhaps you thought I was dead, but I was never better in my life. I am on the ship *Columbia*, bound for San Francisco, around Cape Horn; and just now, as one of the officers tells me, we are off the coast of Brazil.

"There is a ship coming north, and we are going to hail her and give her letters to carry home, so I hope these few lines will reach you all right. I suppose I am in for it, and must keep on to San Francisco. But I haven't told you yet how I came here.

"It was through a trick of your cousin, Curtis Waring. I haven't time to tell you about it; but I was drugged and brought aboard in my sleep; when I woke up I was forty miles at sea.

"Don't worry about me, for I have a good friend on board, Mr. Randolph Leslie, who has been a reporter on one of the New York daily papers. He advises me to get something to do in San Francisco, and work till I have earned money enough to get home. He says I can do better there, where I am not known, and can get higher pay. He is giving me lessons every day, and he says I am learning fast.

"The ship is almost here, and I must stop. Take good care of yourself, and remember me to Mrs. O'Keefe, and I will write you again as soon as I get to San Francisco.

"Dodger.

"P. S. - Don't let on to Curtis that you have heard from me, or he might try to play me some trick in San Francisco."

Florence's face was radiant when she had read the letter.

Dodger was alive, well, and in good spirits. The letter arrived during the afternoon, and she put on her street dress at once and went over to the apple-stand and read the letter to Mrs. O'Keefe.

"Well, well!" ejaculated the apple-woman. "So it's that ould thafe of the worruld, Curtis Waring, that has got hold of poor Dodger, just as Tim told us. It seems mighty quare to me that he should want to stale poor Dodger. If it was you, now, I could understand it."

"It seems strange to me, Mrs. O'Keefe," said Florence, thoughtfully. "I thought it might be because Dodger was my friend, but that doesn't seem to be sufficient explanation. Don't you think we ought to show this letter to Mr. Bolton?"

"I was going to suggest that same. If you'll give it to me, Florence, I'll get Mattie to tend my stand, and slip round wid it to Tim's right off."

"I will go with you, Mrs. O'Keefe."

Mattie, who was playing around the corner, was summoned.

"Now, Mattie, just mind the stand, and don't be runnin' away, or them boys will get away wid my whole mornin's profits. Do you hear?"

"Yes, mum."

"And don't you be eatin' all the while you are here. Here's one apple you can have," and the apple-woman carefully picked out one that she considered unsalable.

"That's specked, Mrs. O'Keefe," objected Mattie.

"And what if it is? Can't you bite out the specks? The rest of the apple is good. You're gettin' mighty particular."

Mattie bit a piece out of the sound part of the apple, and, when Mrs. O'Keefe was at a safe distance, gave the rest to a lame bootblack, and picked out one of the best apples for her own eating.

"Bridget O'Keefe is awful mane wid her apples!" soliloquized Mattie, "but I'm too smart for her. Tryin' to pass off one of her old specked apples on me! If I don't take three good one I'm a sinner."

Arrived at the front of the saloon, Mrs. O'Keefe penetrated the interior, and met Tim near the door.

"Have you come in for some whiskey, old lady?" asked Tim, in a jesting tone.

"I'll take that by and by. Florence is outside, and we've got some news for you."

"Won't she come in?"

"No; she don't like to be seen in a place like this. She's got a letter from Dodger."

"You don't mean it!" ejaculated Tim, with sudden interest. "Where is he?"

"Come out and see."

"Good afternoon, Miss Linden," said Tim, gallantly. "So you've news from Dodger?"

"Yes; here is the letter."

Bolton read it through attentively.

"Curtis is smart," he said, as he handed it back. "He couldn't have thought of a better plan for getting rid of the boy. It will take several months for him to reach 'Frisco, and after that he can't get back, for he won't have any money."

"Dodger says he will try to save money enough to pay his way back."

"It will take him a good while."

"It doesn't take long to come back by cars, does it?"

"No; but it costs a great deal of money. Why, it may take Dodger a year to earn enough to pay his way back on the railroad."

"A year!" exclaimed Florence, in genuine dismay - "a year, in addition to the time it takes to go out there! Where will we all be at the end of that time?"

"Not in jail, I hope," answered Bolton, jocularly. "I am afraid your uncle will no longer be in the land of the living."

A shadow came over Florence's face.

"Poor Uncle John!" she said, sadly. "It is terrible to think he may die thinking hardly of me."

"Leavin' his whole fortune to Curtis," continued Tim.

"That is the least thing that troubles me," said Florence.

"A woman's a queer thing," said Tim, shrugging his shoulders. "Here's a fortune of maybe half a million, and half of it rightfully yours, and you don't give it a thought."

"Not compared with the loss of my uncle's affections."

"Money is a great deal more practical than affection."

"Perhaps so, from your standpoint, Mr. Bolton," said Florence, with dignity.

"No offense, miss. When you've lived as long as I, you'll look at things different. Well, I'm glad to hear from the lad. If Curtis had done him any harm, I'd have got even with him if it sent me to jail."

A quiet, determined look replaced Tim Bolton's usual expression of easy good humor. He could not have said anything that would have ingratiated him more with Florence.

"Thank you, Mr. Bolton," she said, earnestly. "I shall always count upon your help. I believe you are a true friend of Dodger -"

"And of yours, too, miss -"

"I believe it," she said, with a smile that quite captivated Tim.

"If it would be any satisfaction to you, Miss Florence," he continued, "I'll give Curtis Waring a lickin'. He deserves it for persecutin' you and gettin' you turned out of your uncle's house."

"Thank you, Mr. Bolton; it wouldn't be any satisfaction to me to see Curtis injured in any way."

"You're too good a Christian, you are, Miss Florence."

"I wish I deserved your praise, but I can hardly lay claim to it. Now, Mr. Bolton, tell me what can I do to help Dodger?"

"I don't see that you can do anything now, as it will be most three months before he reaches 'Frisco. You might write to him toward the time he gets there."

"I will."

"Direct to the post office. I think he'll have sense enough to ask for letters."

"I wish I could send him some money. I am afraid he will land penniless."

"If he lands in good health you can trust him for makin' a livin'. A New York boy, brought up as he was, isn't goin' to starve where there are papers to sell and errands to run. Why, he'll light on his feet in 'Frisco, take my word for it."

Florence felt a good deal encouraged by Tim's words of assurance, and she went home with her heart perceptibly lightened.

But she was soon to have trials of her own, which for the time being would make her forgetful of Dodger.

CHAPTER XXIX

MRS. LEIGHTON'S PARTY

"Miss Linden," said Mrs. Leighton, one day in the fourth month of Dodger's absence, "Carrie has perhaps told you that I give a party next Thursday evening."

"She told me," answered the governess.

"I expected Prof. Bouvier to furnish dancing music - in fact, I had engaged him - but I have just received a note stating that he is unwell, and I am left unprovided. It is very inconsiderate on his part," added the lady, in a tone of annoyance.

Florence did not reply. She took rather a different view of the professor's letter, and did not care to offend Mrs. Leighton.

"Under the circumstances," continued the lady, "it has occurred to me that, as you are really quite a nice performer, you might fill his place. I shall be willing to allow you a dollar for the evening. What do you say?"

Florence felt embarrassed. She shrank from appearing in society in her present separation from her family, yet could think of no good excuse. Noticing her hesitation, Mrs. Leighton added, patronizingly:

"On second thought, I will pay you a dollar and a half" - Prof. Bouvier was to have charged ten dollars - "and you will be kind enough to come in your best attire. You seem to be well provided with dresses."

"Yes, madam, there will be no difficulty on that score."

"Nor on any other, I hope. As governess in my family, I think I have a right to command your services."

"I will come," said Florence, meekly. She felt that it would not do to refuse after this.

As she entered the handsomely decorated rooms on the night of the party, she looked around her nervously, fearing to see some one whom she had known in earlier days. She noticed one only - Percy de Brabazon, whose face lighted up when he saw her, for he had been expecting to see her.

She managed to convey a caution by a quiet movement, as it would not be wise for Mrs. Leighton to know of their previous acquaintance. But Percy was determined to get an opportunity to speak to her.

"Who is that young lady, Aunt Mary?" he asked. "The one standing near the piano."

"That is Carrie's governess," answered Mrs. Leighton, carelessly.

"She seems quite a ladylike person."

"Yes. I understand she has seen better days. She is to play for us in the absence of Prof. Bouvier."

"Will you introduce me, aunt?"

"Why?" asked Mrs. Leighton, with a searching look.

"I should like to inquire about Carrie's progress in her studies," said the cunning Percy.

"Oh, certainly," answered the aunt, quite deceived by his words.

"Miss Linden," she said, "let me introduce my nephew, Mr. de Brabazon. He wishes to inquire about Carrie's progress in her studies."

And the lady sailed off to another part of the room.

"I can assure you, Mr. de Brabazon," said Florence, "that my young charge is making excellent progress."

"I can easily believe it, under your instruction," said Percy.

"I am very glad you take such an interest in your cousin," added Florence, with a smile. "It does you great credit."

"It's only an excuse, you know, to get a chance to talk with you, Miss Linden. May I say Miss Florence?"

"No," answered Florence, decidedly. "It won't do. You must be very formal."

"Then tell me how you like teaching."

"Very well, indeed."

"It must be an awful bore, I think."

"I don't think so. Carrie is a warm-hearted, affectionate girl. Besides, she is very bright and gives me very little trouble."

"Don't you think you could take another pupil, Miss Linden?"

"A young girl?"

"No, a young man. In fact, myself."

"What could I teach you, Mr. de Brabazon?"

"Lots of things. I am not very sound in - in spelling and grammar."

"What a pity!" answered Florence, with mock seriousness. "I am afraid your aunt would hardly consent to have a boy of your size in the schoolroom."

"Then perhaps you could give me some private lessons in the afternoon?"

"That would not be possible."

Just then Mrs. Leighton came up.

"Well," she said, "what does Miss Linden say of Carrie?"

"She has quite satisfied my mind about her," answered Percy, with excusable duplicity. "I think her methods are excellent. I was telling her that I might be able to procure her another pupil."

"I have no objection, as long as it does not interfere with Carrie's hours. Miss Linden, there is a call for music. Will you go to the piano and play a Stauss waltz?"

Florence inclined her head obediently.

"Let me escort you to the piano, Miss Linden," said Percy.

"Thank you," answered Florence, in a formal tone.

For an hour Florence was engaged in playing waltzes, gallops and lanciers music. Then a lady who was proud of her daughter's proficiency volunteered her services to relieve Florence.

"Now you can dance yourself," said Percy, in a low tone. "Will you give me a waltz?"

"Not at once. Wait till the second dance."

Percy de Brabazon was prompt in presenting himself as soon as permitted, and he led Florence out for a dance.

Both were excellent dancers, and attracted general attention.

Florence really enjoyed dancing, and forgot for a time that she was only a guest on sufferance, as she moved with rhythmic grace about the handsome rooms.

Percy was disposed to prolong the dance, but Florence was cautious.

"I think I will rest now, Mr. de Brabazon," she said.

"You will favor me again later in the evening?" he pleaded.

"I hardly think it will be wise."

But when, half an hour later, he asked her again, Florence could not find it in her heart to say no. It would have been wise if she had done so. A pair of jealous eyes was fixed upon her. Miss Emily Carter had for a considerable time tried to fascinate Mr. de Brabazon, whose wealth made him a very desirable match, and she viewed his decided penchant for Florence with alarm and indignation.

"To be thrown in the shade by a governess is really too humiliating!" she murmured to herself in vexation. "If it were a girl in my own station I should not care so much," and she eyed Florence with marked hostility.

"Mamma," she said, "do you see how Mr. de Barbazon is carrying on with Mrs. Leighton's governess? Really, I think it very discreditable."

Mrs. Carter looked through her gold eye-glasses at the couple.

"Is the girl really a governess?" she added. "She is very well dressed."

"I don't know where she got her dress, but she is really a governess."

"She seems very bold."

"So she does."

Poor Florence! She was far from deserving their unkindly remarks.

"I suppose she is trying to ensnare young de Brabazon," said Emily, spitefully. "People of her class are very artful. Don't you think it would be well to call Mrs. Leighton's attention? Percy de Brabazon is her nephew, you know."

"True. The suggestion is a good one, Emily."

Mrs. Carter was quite as desirous as her daughter of bringing about an alliance with Percy, and she readily agreed to second her plans.

She looked about for Mrs. Leighton, and took a seat at her side.

"Your nephew seems quite attentive to your governess," she commenced.

"Indeed! In what way?"

"He has danced with her three or four times, I believe. It looks rather marked."

"So it does," said Mrs. Leighton. "He is quite inconsiderate."

"Oh, well, it is of no great consequence. She is quite stylish for a governess, and doubtless your nephew is taken with her."

"That will not suit my views at all," said Mrs.

Leighton, coldly. "I shall speak to her to-morrow."

"Pray don't. It really is a matter of small consequence - quite natural, in fact."

"Leave the matter with me. You have done quite right in mentioning it."

At twelve o'clock the next day, when Florence had just completed her lessons with Carrie, Mrs. Leighton entered the room.

"Please remain a moment, Miss Linden," she said. "I have a few words to say to you."

Mrs. Leighton's tone was cold and unfriendly, and Florence felt that something unpleasant was coming.

CHAPTER XXX

FLORENCE IS FOLLOWED HOME

"I am listening, madam," said Florence, inclining her head.

"I wish to speak to you about last evening, Miss Linden."

"I hope my playing was satisfactory, Mrs. Leighton. I did my best."

"I have no fault to find with your music. It came up to my expectations."

"I am glad of that, madam."

"I referred, rather, to your behavior, Miss Linden."

"I don't understand you, Mrs. Leighton," Florence responded, in unaffected surprise. "Please explain."

"You danced several times with my nephew, Mr. Percy de Brabazon."

"Twice, madam."

"I understood it was oftener. However, that is

immaterial. You hardly seemed conscious of your position."

"What was my position, Mrs. Leighton?" asked Florence, quietly, looking her employer in the face. "Well - ahem!" answered Mrs. Leighton, a little ill at ease, "you were a hired musician."

"Well?"

"And you acted as if you were an invited guest."

"I am sorry you did not give me instructions as to my conduct," said the governess, coldly. "I should not have danced if I had been aware that it was prohibited."

"I am sorry, Miss Linden, that you persist in misunderstanding me. Mr. de Brabazon, being in a different social position from yourself, it looked hardly proper that he should have devoted himself to you more than to any other lady."

"Did he? I was not aware of it. Don't you think, under the circumstances, that he is the one whom you should take to task? I didn't invite his attentions."

"You seemed glad to receive them."

"I was. He is undoubtedly a gentleman."

"Certainly he is. He is my nephew."

"It was not my part to instruct him as to what was proper, surely."

"You are very plausible. Miss Linden, I think it right to tell you that your conduct was commented upon by one of my lady guests as unbecoming. However, I will remember, in extenuation, that you are unaccustomed to society, and doubtless erred ignorantly."

Florence bowed, but forbore to make any remark.

"Do you wish to speak further to me, Mrs. Leighton?"

"No, I think not."

"Then I will bid you good-morning."

When the governess had left the house, Mrs. Leighton asked herself whether in her encounter with her governess the victory rested with her, and she was forced to acknowledge that it was at least a matter of doubt.

"Miss Linden is a faithful teacher, but she does not appear to appreciate the difference that exists between her and my guests. I think, however, that upon reflection, she will see that I am right in my stricture upon her conduct."

Florence left the house indignant and mortified. It was something new to her to be regarded as a social inferior, and she felt sure that there were many in Mrs. Leighton's position who would have seen no harm in her behavior on the previous evening.

Four days afterward, when Florence entered the Madison Avenue car to ride downtown, she had scarcely reached her seat when an eager voice addressed her:

"Miss Linden, how fortunate I am in meeting you!"

Florence looked up and saw Mr. de Brabazon sitting nearly opposite her.

Though she felt an esteem for him, she was sorry to see him, for, with Mrs. Leighton's rebuke fresh in her mind, it could only be a source of embarrassment, and, if discovered, subject her in all probability to a fresh reprimand.

"You are kind to say so, Mr. de Brabazon."

"Not at all. I hoped I might meet you again soon. What a pleasant time we had at the party."

"I thought so at the time, but the next day I changed my mind."

"Why, may I ask?"

"Because your aunt, Mrs. Leighton, took me to task for dancing with you twice."

"Was she so absurd?" ejaculated Percy.

"It is not necessarily absurd. She said our social positions were so different that it was unbecoming for me to receive attention from you."

"Rubbish!" exclaimed Percy, warmly.

"I am afraid I ought not to listen to such strictures upon the words of my employer."

"I wish you didn't have to teach."

"I can't join you in that wish. I enjoy my work."

"But you ought to be relieved from the necessity."

"We must accept things as we find them," said Florence, gravely.

"There is a way out of it," said Percy, quickly. "You understand me, do you not?"

"I think I do, Mr. de Brabazon, and I am grateful to you, but I am afraid it can never be."

Percy remained silent.

"How far are you going?" asked Florence, uneasily, for she did not care to have her companion learn where she lived.

"I intend to get out at Fourteenth Street."

"Then I must bid you good-afternoon, for we are already at Fifteenth Street."

"If I can be of any service to you, I will ride farther."

"Thank you," said Florence, hastily, "but it is quite unnecessary."

"Then, good morning!"

And Percy descended from the car.

In another part of the car sat a young lady, who listened with sensations far from pleasant to the conversation that had taken place between Florence and Mr. de Brabazon.

It was Emily Carter, whose jealousy had been excited on the evening of the party. She dropped her veil, fearing to be recognized by Mr. de Brabazon, with whom she was well acquainted. She, too, had intended getting off at Fourteenth Street, but decided to remain longer in the car.

"I will find out where that girl lives," she resolved. "Her conduct with Percy de Brabazon is positively disgraceful. She is evidently doing her best to captivate him. I feel that it is due to Mrs. Leighton, who would be shocked at the thought of her nephew's making a low alliance, to find out all I can, and put her on her guard."

She kept her seat, still keeping her veil down, for it was possible that Florence might recognize her; and the car moved steadily onward till it turned into the Bowery.

"Where on earth is she leading me?" Miss Carter asked herself. "I have never been in this neighborhood before. However, it won't do to give up, when I am, perhaps, on the verge of some important discoveries."

Still the car sped on. Not far from Grand Street, Florence left the car, followed, though she was unconscious of it, by her aristocratic fellow-passenger.

Florence stopped a moment to speak to Mrs. O'Keefe at her apple-stand.

"So you're through wid your work, Florence. Are you goin' home?"

"Yes, Mrs. O'Keefe."

"Then I'll go wid you, for I've got a nasty headache, and I'll lie down for an hour."

They crossed the street, not noticing the veiled young lady, who followed within ear shot, and listened to their conversation. At length they reached the tenement house - Florence's humble home - and went in.

"I've learned more than I bargained for," said Emily Carter, in malicious exultation. "I am well repaid for coming to this horrid part of the city. I wonder if Mr. de Brabazon knows where his charmer lives? I will see that Mrs. Leighton knows, at any rate."

CHAPTER XXXI

FLORENCE IS DISCHARGED

Mrs. Leighton sat in her boudoir with a stern face and tightly compressed lips. Miss Carter had called the previous afternoon and informed her of the astounding discoveries she had made respecting the governess.

She rang the bell.

"Janet," she said, "when the governess comes you may bring her up here to me."

"Yes, ma'am."

"She's going to catch it - I wonder what for?" thought Janet, as she noted the grim visage of her employer.

So when Florence entered the house she was told that Mrs. Leighton wished to see her at once.

"I wonder what's the matter now?" she asked herself. "Has she heard of my meeting her nephew in the car?"

When she entered the room she saw at once that something was wrong.

"You wished to see me, Mrs. Leighton?" she said.

"Yes," answered Mrs. Leighton, grimly. "Will you be seated?"

Florence sat down a few feet from her employer and waited for an explanation.

She certainly was not prepared for Mrs. Leighton's first words:

"Miss Linden, where do you live?"

Florence started, and her face flushed.

"I live in the lower part of the city," she answered, with hesitation.

"That is not sufficiently definite."

"I live at No. 27 - Street."

"I think that is east of the Bowery."

"You are right, madam."

"You lodge with an apple-woman, do you not?"

"I do," answered Florence, calmly.

"In a tenement house?"

"Yes, madam."

"And you actually come from such a squalid home to instruct my daughter!" exclaimed Mrs. Leighton, indignantly. "It is a wonder you have not brought some terrible disease into the house."

"There has been no case of disease in the humble dwelling in which I make my home. I should be as sorry to expose your daughter to any danger of that kind as you would be to have me."

"It is a merciful dispensation of Providence, for which I ought to be truly thankful. But the idea of receiving in my house an inmate of a tenement house! I am truly shocked. Is this apple-woman your mother?"

"I assure you that she is not," answered Florence, with a smile which she could not repress.

"Or your aunt?"

"She is in no way related to me. She is an humble friend.

"Miss Linden, your tastes must be low to select such a home and such a friend."

"The state of my purse had something to do with the selection, and the kindness shown me by Mrs. O'Keefe, when I needed a friend, will explain my location further."

"That is not all. You met in the Madison Avenue car yesterday my nephew, Mr. Percy de Brabazon."

"It is coming," thought Florence. "Who could have seen us?" Then aloud:

"Yes, madam."

"Was it by appointment?"

"Do you mean to insult me, Mrs. Leighton?" demanded Florence, rising and looking at the lady with flashing eyes.

"I never insult anybody," replied Mrs. Leighton. "Pray, resume your seat."

Florence did so.

"Then I may assume that it was accidental. You talked together with the freedom of old friends?"

"You are correctly informed."

"You seem to make acquaintances very readily, Miss Linden. It seems singular, to say the least, that after meeting my nephew for a single evening, you should become such intimate friends."

"You will be surprised, Mrs. Leighton, when I say that Mr. de Brabazon and I are old friends. We have met frequently."

"Where, in Heaven's name?" ejaculated Mrs. Leighton.

"At my residence."

"Good Heavens!" exclaimed the scandalized lady. "Does my nephew Percy visit at the house of this apple-woman?"

"No, madam. He does not know where I live."

"Then you will explain your previous statement?" said Mrs. Leighton, haughtily.

"I am at present suffering reversed circumstances. It is but a short time since I was very differently situated."

"I won't inquire into your change of circumstances. I feel compelled to perform an unpleasant duty."

Florence did not feel called upon to make any reply, but waited for Mrs. Leighton to finish speaking.

"I shall be obliged to dispense with your services as my daughter's governess. It is quite out of the question for me to employ a person who lives in a tenement-house."

Florence bowed acquiescence, but she felt very sad. She had become attached to her young charge, and it cost her a pang to part from her.

Besides, how was she to supply the income of which this would deprive her?

"I bow to your decision, madam," she said, with proud humility.

"You will find here the sum that I owe you, with payment for an extra week in lieu of notice."

"Thank you. May I bid Carrie good-by, Mrs. Leighton?"

"It is better not to do so, I think. The more quietly we dissolve our unfortunate connection the better!"

Florence's heart swelled, and the tears came to her eyes, but she could not press her request.

She was destined, however, to obtain the privilege which Mrs. Leighton denied her. Carrie, who had become impatient, came downstairs and burst into the room.

"What keeps you so long, Miss Linden?" she said. "Is mamma keeping you?"

Florence was silent, leaving the explanations to Mrs. Leighton.

"Miss Linden has resigned her position as your governess, Carrie."

"Miss Linden going away! I won't have her go! What makes you go, Miss Linden?"

"Your mamma thinks it best," answered Florence, with moistened eyes.

"Well, I don't!" exclaimed Carrie, stamping her foot, angrily. "I won't have any other governess but you."

"Carrie, you are behaving very unbecomingly," said her mother.

"Will you tell me, mamma, why you are sending Miss Linden away?"

"I will tell you some other time."

"But I want to know now."

"I am very much displeased with you, Carrie."

"And I am very much displeased with you, mamma."

I do not pretend to defend Carrie, whose conduct was hardly respectful enough to her mother; but with all her faults she had a warm heart, while her mother had always been cold and selfish.

"I am getting tired of this," said Mrs. Leighton. "Miss Linden, as you are here to-day, you may give Carrie the usual lessons. As I shall be out when you get through, I bid you good-by now."

"Good-by, Mrs. Leighton."

Carrie and Florence went to the schoolroom for the last time.

Florence gave her young pupil a partial explanation of the cause which had led to her discharge.

"What do I care if you live in a poor house, Miss Linden?" said Carrie, impetuously. "I will make mamma take you back!"

Florence smiled; but she knew that there would be no return for her.

When she reached her humble home she had a severe headache and lay down. Mrs. O'Keefe came in later to see her.

"And what's the matter with you, Florence?" she asked.

"I have a bad headache, Mrs. O'Keefe."

"You work too hard, Florence, wid your teacher. That is what gives you the headache."

"Then I shan't have it again, for I have got through with my teaching."

"What's that you say?"

"I am discharged."

"And what's it all about?"

Florence explained matters. Mrs. O'Keefe became indignant.

"She's a mean trollop, that Mrs. Leighton!" she exclaimed, "and I'd like to tell her so to her face. Where does she live?"

"It will do no good to interfere, my good friend. She is not willing to receive a governess from a tenement house."

"Shure you used to live in as grand a house as herself."

"But I don't now."

"Don't mind it too much, mavoureen. You'll soon be gettin' another scholar. Go to sleep now, and you'll sleep the headache away."

Florence finally succeeded in following the advice of her humble friend.

She resolved to leave till the morrow the cares of the morrow.

She had twelve dollars, and before that was spent she hoped to be in a position to earn some more.

CHAPTER XXXII

AN EXCITING ADVENTURE

Dodger soon became accustomed to his duties at Tucker's express office, in his new San Francisco home. He found Mr. Tucker an exacting, but not an unreasonable, man. He watched his new assistant closely for the first few days, and was quietly taking his measure.

At the end of the first week he paid the salary agreed upon - fifteen dollars.

"You have been with me a week, Arthur," he said.

"Yes, sir."

"And I have been making up my mind about you."

"Yes, sir," said Dodger, looking up inquiringly. "I hope you are satisfied with me?"

"Yes, I think I may say that I am. You don't seem to be afraid of work."

"I have always been accustomed to work."

"That is well. I was once induced to take the son of a

rich man in the place you now occupy. He had never done a stroke of work, having always been at school. He didn't take kindly to work, and seemed afraid that he would be called upon to do more than he had bargained for. One evening I was particularly busy, and asked him to remain an hour overtime.

"'It will be very inconvenient, Mr. Tucker,' said the young man, 'as I have an engagement with a friend.'

"He left me to do all the extra work, and - I suppose you know what happened the next Saturday evening?"

"I can guess," returned Dodger, with a smile.

"I told him that I thought the duties were too heavy for his constitution, and he had better seek an easier place. Let me see - I kept you an hour and a half overtime last Wednesday."

"Yes, sir."

"You made no objection, but worked on just as if you liked it."

"Yes, sir; I am always willing to stay when you need me."

"Good! I shan't forget it."

Dodger felt proud of his success, and put away the fifteen dollars with a feeling of satisfaction. He had never saved half that sum in the same time before.

"Curtis Waring did me a favor when he sent me out here," he reflected; "but as he didn't mean it, I have no occasion to feel grateful."

Dodger found that he could live for eight dollars a week, and he began to lay by seven dollars a week with the view of securing funds sufficient to take him back to New York.

He was in no hurry to leave San Francisco, but he felt that Florence might need a friend. But he found that he was making progress slowly.

At that time the price of a first-class ticket to New York was one hundred and twenty-eight dollars, besides the expense of sleeping berths, amounting then, as now, to twenty-two dollars extra. So it looked as if Dodger would be compelled to wait at least six months before he should be in a position to set out on the return journey.

About this time Dodger received a letter from Florence, in which she spoke of her discharge by Mrs. Leighton.

"I shall try to obtain another position as teacher," she said, concealing her anxiety. "I am sure, in a large city, I can find something to do."

But Dodger knew better than she the difficulties that beset the path of an applicant for work, and he could not help feeling anxious for Florence.

"If I were only in New York," he said to himself, "I would see that Florence didn't suffer. I will write her to let me know if she is in need, and I will send her some money."

About this time he met with an adventure which deserves to be noted.

It was about seven o'clock one evening that he found himself in Mission Street.

At a street corner his attention was drawn to a woman poorly dressed, who held by the hand a child of three.

Her clothing was shabby, and her attitude was one of despondency. It was clear that she was ill and in trouble.

Dodger possessed quick sympathies, and his own experience made him quick to understand and feel for the troubles of others.

Though the woman made no appeal, he felt instinctively that she needed help.

"I beg your pardon," he said, with as much deference as if he were addressing one favored by fortune, "but you seem to be in need of help?"

"God knows, I am!" said the woman, sadly.

"Perhaps I can be of service to you. Will you tell me how?"

"Neither I nor my child has tasted food since yesterday."

"Well, that can be easily remedied," said Dodger, cheerfully. "There is a restaurant close by. I was about to eat supper. Will you come in with me?"

"I am ashamed to impose upon the kindness of a stranger," murmured the woman.

"Don't mention it. I shall be very glad of company," said Dodger, heartily.

"But you are a poor boy. You may be ill able to afford the expense."

"I am not a millionaire," said Dodger, "and I don't see any immediate prospect of my building a palace on Nob Hill" - where live some of San Francisco's wealthiest citizens - "but I am very well supplied with money."

"Then I will accept your kind invitation."

It was a small restaurant, but neat in its appointments, and, as in most San Francisco restaurants, the prices were remarkably moderate.

At an expense of twenty-five cents each, the three obtained a satisfactory meal.

The woman and child both seemed to enjoy it, and Dodger was glad to see that the former became more cheerful as time went on.

There was something in the child's face that looked familiar to Dodger. It was a resemblance to some one that he had seen, but he could not for the life of him decide who it was.

"How can I ever thank you for your kindness?" said the lady, as she arose from the table. "You don't know what it is to be famished -"

"Don't I?" asked Dodger. "I have been hungry more than once, without money enough to buy a meal."

"You don't look it," she said.

"No, for now I have a good place and am earning a good salary."

"Are you a native of San Francisco?"

"No, madam. I can't tell you where I was born, for I know little or nothing of my family. I have only been here a short time. I came from New York."

"So did I," said the woman, with a sigh. "I wish I were back there again."

"How came you to be here? Don't answer if you prefer not to," Dodger added, hastily.

"I have no objection. My husband deserted me, and left me to shift for myself and support my child."

"How have you done it?"

"By taking in sewing. But that is a hard way of earning money. There are too many poor women who are ready to work for starvation wages, and so we all suffer."

"I know that," answered Dodger. "Do you live near here?"

The woman mentioned a street near by.

"I have one poor back room on the third floor," she

explained; "but I should be glad if I were sure to stay there."

"Is there any danger of your being ejected?"

"I am owing for two weeks' rent, and this is the middle of the third week. Unless I can pay up at the end of this week I shall be forced to go out into the streets with my poor child."

"How much rent do you pay?"

"A dollar a week."

"Then three dollars will relieve you for the present?"

"Yes; but it might as well be three hundred," said the woman, bitterly.

"Not quite; I can supply you with three dollars, but three hundred would be rather beyond my means."

"You are too kind, too generous! I ought not to accept such a liberal gift."

"Mamma, I am tired. Take me up in your arms," said the child.

"Poor child! He has been on his feet all day," sighed the mother.

She tried to lift the child, but her own strength had been undermined by privation, and she was clearly unable to do so.

"Let me take him!" said Dodger. "Here, little one,

jump up!"

He raised the child easily, and despite the mother's protest, carried him in his arms.

"I will see you home, madam," he said.

"I fear the child will be too heavy for you."

"I hope not. Why, I could carry a child twice as heavy."

They reached the room at last - a poor one, but a welcome repose from the streets.

"Don't you ever expect to see your husband again?" asked Dodger. "Can't you compel him to support you?"

"I don't know where he is," answered the woman, despondently.

"If you will tell me his name, I may come across him some day."

"His name," said the woman, "is Curtis Waring."

Dodger stared at her, overwhelmed with surprise.

CHAPTER XXXIII

AN IMPORTANT DISCOVERY

"Curtis Waring!" ejaculated Dodger, his face showing intense surprise. "Is that the name of your husband?"

"Yes. Is it possible that you know him?" asked the woman, struck by Dodger's tone.

"I know a man by that name. I will describe him, and you can tell me whether it is he. He is rather tall, dark hair, sallow complexion, black eyes, and a long, thin nose."

"It is like him in every particular. Oh, tell me where he is to be found?"

"He lives in New York. He is the nephew of a rich man, and is expecting to inherit his wealth. Through his influence a cousin of his, a young lady, has been driven from home."

"Was he afraid she would deprive him of the estate?"

"That was partly the reason. But it was partly to revenge himself on her because she would not agree to marry him."

"But how could he marry her," exclaimed the unfortunate woman, "when he is already married to me?"

"Neither she nor any one of his family or friends knew that he was already married. I don't think it would trouble him much."

"But it must be stopped!" she exclaimed, wildly. "He is my husband. I shall not give him up to any one else."

"So far as Florence is concerned - she is the cousin - she has no wish to deprive you of him. But is it possible that you are attached to a man who has treated you so meanly?" asked Dodger, in surprise.

"There was a time when he treated me well, when he appeared to love me," was the murmured reply. "I cannot forget that he is the father of my child."

Dodger did not understand the nature of women or the mysteries of the female heart, and he evidently thought this poor woman very foolish to cling with such pertinacity to a man like Curtis Waring.

"Do you mind telling me how you came to marry him?" he asked.

"It was over four years ago that I met him in this city," was the reply. "I am a San Francisco girl. I had never been out of California. I was considered pretty then," she added, with a remnant of pride, "faded as I am to-day."

Looking closely in her face, Dodger was ready to believe this.

Grief and privation had changed her appearance, but it had not altogether effaced the bloom and beauty of youth.

"At any rate, he seemed to think so. He was living at the Palace Hotel, and I made his acquaintance at a small social gathering at the house of my uncle. I am an orphan, and was perhaps the more ready to marry on that account."

"Did Mr. Waring represent himself as wealthy?"

"He said he had expectations from a wealthy relative, but did not mention where he lived."

"He told the truth, then."

"We married, securing apartments on Kearney Street. We lived together till my child was born, and for three months afterward. Then Mr. Waring claimed to be called away from San Francisco on business. He said he might be absent six weeks. He left me a hundred dollars, and urged me to be careful of it, as he was short of money, and needed considerable for the expenses of the journey. He left me, and I have never seen or heard from him since."

"Did he tell you where he was going, Mrs. Waring?"

"No; he said he would be obliged to visit several places - among others, Colorado, where he claimed to have some mining property. He told me that he hoped to bring back considerable money."

"Do you think he meant to stay away altogether?"

"I don't know what to think. Well, I lived on patiently, for I had perfect confidence in my husband. I made the money last me ten weeks instead of six, but then I found myself penniless."

"Did you receive any letters in that time?"

"No, and it was that that worried me. When at last the money gave out, I began to pawn my things - more than once I was tempted to pawn my wedding-ring, but I could not bring my mind to do that. I do not like to think ill of my husband, and was forced, as the only alternative, to conclude that he had met with some accident, perhaps had died. I have not felt certain that this was not so till you told me this evening that you know him."

"I can hardly say that I know him well, yet I know him a good deal better than I wish I did. But for him I would not now be in San Francisco."

"How is that? Please explain."

Dodger told her briefly the story of his abduction.

"But what motive could he have in getting you out of New York? I cannot understand."

"I don't understand myself, except that I am the friend of Florence."

"His cousin?"

"Yes."

"But why should she be compelled to leave her

uncle's home?"

"Because Curtis Waring made him set his heart upon the match. She had her choice to marry Curtis or to leave the house, and forfeit all chance of the estate. She chose to leave the house."

"She ought to know that he has no right to marry," said the poor woman, who, not understanding the dislike of Florence for the man whom she herself loved, feared that she might yet be induced to marry him.

"She ought to know, and her uncle ought to know," said Dodger. "Mrs. Waring, I can't see my way clear yet. If I were in New York I would know just what to do. Will you agree to stand by me, and help me?"

"Yes, I will," answered the woman, earnestly.

"I will see you again to-morrow evening. Here is some money to help you along for the present. Good-night."

Dodger, as he walked away, pondered over the remarkable discovery he had made.

It was likely to prove of the utmost importance to Florence.

Her uncle's displeasure was wholly based upon her refusal to marry Curtis Waring, but if it should be proved to him that Curtis was already a married man, there would seem no bar to reconciliation.

Moreover - and thas was particularly satisfactory - it would bring Curtis himself into disfavor.

Florence would be reinstated in her rightful place in her uncle's family, and once more be recognized as heiress to at least a portion of his large fortune.

This last consideration might not weigh so much with Florence, but Dodger was more practical, and he wished to restore her to the social position which she had lost through the knavery of her cousin.

But in San Francisco - at a distance of over three thousand miles - Dodger felt at a loss how to act.

Even if Mr. Linden was informed that his nephew had a wife living in San Francisco, the statement would no doubt be denied by Curtis, who would brand the woman as an impudent adventuress.

"The absent are always in the wrong," says a French proverb.

At all events, they are very much at a disadvantage, and therefore it seemed imperatively necessary, not only that Dodger, but that Curtis Waring's wife should go to New York to confront the unprincipled man whose schemes had brought sorrow to so many.

It was easy to decide what plan was best, but how to carry it out presented a difficulty which seemed insurmountable.

The expenses of a journey to New York for Dodger, Mrs. Waring and her child would not be very far from five hundred dollars, and where to obtain this money was a problem.

Randolph Leslie probably had that sum, but Dodger

could not in conscience ask him to lend it, being unable to furnish adequate security, or to insure repayment.

"If I could only find a nugget," thought Dodger, knitting his brows, "everything would be easy." But nuggets are rare enough in the gold fields, and still rarer in city streets.

He who trusts wholly to luck trusts to a will-o'-the-wisp, and is about as sure of success as one who owns a castle in Spain.

The time might come when Dodger, by his own efforts, could accumulate the needed sum, but it would require a year at least, and in that time Mr. Linden would probably be dead.

Absorbed and disturbed by these reflections, Dodger walked slowly through the darkened streets till he heard a stifled cry, and looking up, beheld a sight that startled him.

On the sidewalk lay the prostrate figure of a man. Over him, bludgeon in hand, bent a ruffian, whose purpose was only too clearly evident.

CHAPTER XXXIV

JUST IN TIME

Dodger, who was a strong, stout boy, gathered himself up and dashed against the ruffian with such impetuosity that he fell over his intended victim, and his bludgeon fell from his hand.

It was the work of an instant to lift it, and raise it in a menacing position.

The discomfited villain broke into a volley of oaths, and proceeded to pick himself up.

He was a brutal-looking fellow, but was no larger than Dodger, who was as tall as the majority of men.

"Give me that stick," he exclaimed, furiously.

"Come and take it," returned Dodger, undaunted.

The fellow took him at his word, and made a rush at our hero, but a vigorous blow from the bludgeon made him cautious about repeating the attack.

"Curse you!" he cried, between his teeth. "I'd like to chaw you up."

"I have no doubt you would," answered Dodger; "but I don't think you will. Were you going to rob this man?"

"None of your business!"

"I shall make it my business. You'd better go, or you may be locked up."

"Give me that stick, then."

"You'll have to do without it."

He made another rush, and Dodger struck him such a blow on his arm that he winced with pain.

"Now I shall summon the police, and you can do as you please about going."

Dodger struck the stick sharply on the sidewalk three times, and the ruffian, apprehensive of arrest, ran around the corner just in time to rush into the arms of a policeman.

"What has this man been doing?" asked the city guardian, turning to Dodger.

"He was about to rob this man."

"Is the man hurt?"

"Where am I?" asked the prostrate man, in a bewildered tone.

"I will take care of him, if you will take charge of that fellow."

"Can you get up, sir?" asked Dodger, bending over the fallen man.

The latter answered by struggling to his feet and looking about him in a confused way.

"Where am I?" he asked. "What has happened?"

"You were attacked by a ruffian. I found you on the sidewalk, with him bending over you with this club in his hand."

"He must have followed me. I was imprudent enough to show a well-filled pocketbook in a saloon where I stopped to take a drink. No doubt he planned to relieve me of it."

"You have had a narrow escape, sir."

"I have no doubt of it. I presume the fellow was ready to take my life, if he found it necessary."

"I will leave you now, sir, if you think you can manage."

"No, stay with me. I feel rather upset."

"Where are you staying, sir?"

"At the Palace Hotel. Of course you know where that is?"

"Certainly. Will you take my arm?"

"Thank you."

Little was said till they found themselves in the sumptuous hotel, which hardly has an equal in America.

"Come to my room, young man; I want to speak to you."

It was still early in the evening, and Dodger's time was his own.

He had no hesitation, therefore, in accepting the stranger's invitation.

On the third floor the stranger produced a key and opened the door of a large, handsomely-furnished room.

"If you have a match, please light the gas."

Dodger proceeded to do so, and now, for the first time, obtained a good view of the man he had rescued. He was a man of about the average height, probably not far from fifty, dressed in a neat business suit, and looked like a substantial merchant.

"Please be seated."

Dodger sat down in an easy-chair conveniently near him.

"Young man," said the stranger, impressively, "you have done me a great favor."

Dodger felt that this was true, and did not disclaim it.

"I am very glad I came up just as I did," he said.

"How large a sum of money do you think I had about me?" asked his companion.

"Five hundred dollars?"

"Five hundred dollars! Why, that would be a mere trifle."

"It wouldn't be a trifle to me, sir," said Dodger.

"Are you poor?" asked the man, earnestly.

"I have a good situation that pays me fifteen dollars a week, so I ought not to consider myself poor."

"Suppose you had a considerable sum of money given you, what would you do with it?"

"If I had five hundred dollars, I should be able to defeat the schemes of a villain, and restore a young lady to her rights."

"That seems interesting. Tell me the circumstances."

Dodger told the story as briefly as he could. He was encouraged to find that the stranger listened to him with attention.

"Do you know," he said, reflectively, "you have done for me what I once did for another - a rich man? The case was very similar. I was a poor boy at the time. Do you know what he gave me?"

"What was it, sir?"

"A dollar! What do you think of that for generosity?"

"Well, sir, it wasn't exactly liberal. Did you accept it?"

"No. I told him that I didn't wish to inconvenience him. But I asked you how much money you supposed I had. I will tell you. In a wallet I have eleven thousand dollars in bank notes and securities."

"That is a fortune," said Dodger, dazzled at the mention of such a sum.

"If I had lost it, I have plenty more, but the most serious peril was to my life. Through your opportune assistance I have escaped without loss. I fully appreciate the magnitude of the service you have done me. As an evidence of it, please accept these bills."

He drew from the roll two bills and handed them to Dodger.

The boy, glancing at them mechanically, started in amazement. Each bill was for five hundred dollars.

"You have given me a thousand dollars!" he gasped.

"I am aware of it. I consider my life worth that, at least. James Swinton never fails to pay his debts."

"But, sir, a thousand dollars -"

"It's no more than you deserve. When I tell my wife, on my return to Chicago, about this affair, she will blame me for not giving you more."

"You seem to belong to a liberal family, sir."

"I detest meanness, and would rather err on the side of

liberality. Now, if agreeable to you, I will order a bottle of champagne, and solace ourselves for this little incident."

"Thank you, Mr. Swinton, but I have made up my mind not to drink anything stronger than water. I have tended bar in New York, and what I have seen has given me a dislike for liquor of any kind."

"You are a sensible young man. You are right, and I won't urge you. There is my card, and if you ever come to Chicago, call upon me."

"I will, sir."

When Dodger left the Palace Hotel he felt that he was a favorite of fortune.

It is not always that the money we need is so quickly supplied.

He resolved to return to New York as soon as he could manage it, and take with him the wife and child of Curtis Waring.

This would cost him about five hundred dollars, and he would have the same amount left.

Mr. Tucker was reluctant to part with Dodger.

"You are the best assistant I ever had," he said. "I will pay you twenty dollars a week, if that will induce you to stay."

"I would stay if it were not very important for me to return to New York, Mr. Tucker. I do not expect to get a place in New York as good."

"If you come back to San Francisco at any time, I will make a place for you."

"Thank you, sir."

Mrs. Waring was overjoyed when Dodger called upon her and offered to take her back to New York.

"I shall see Curtis again," she said. "How can I ever thank you?"

But Dodger, though unwilling to disturb her dreams of happiness, thought it exceedingly doubtful if her husband would be equally glad to see her.

CHAPTER XXXV

THE DARKEST DAY

When Florence left the employ of Mrs. Leighton she had a few dollars as a reserve fund. As this would not last long, she at once made an effort to obtain employment.

She desired another position as governess, and made application in answer to an advertisement.

Her ladylike manner evidently impressed the lady to whom she applied.

"I suppose you have taught before?" she said.

"Yes, madam."

"In whose family?"

"I taught the daughter of Mrs. Leighton, of West - Street."

"I have heard of the lady. Of course you are at liberty to refer to her?"

"Yes, madam," but there was a hesitation in her tone that excited suspicion.

"Very well; I will call upon her and make inquiries. If you will call to-morrow morning, I can give you a decisive answer."

Florence fervently hoped that this might prove favorable; but was apprehensive, and with good reason, it appeared.

When she presented herself the next day, Mrs. Cole said:

"I am afraid, Miss Linden, you will not suit me."

"May I ask why?" Florence inquired, schooling herself to calmness.

"I called on Mrs. Leighton," was the answer. "She speaks well of you as a teacher, but - she told me some things which make it seem inexpedient to engage you."

"What did she say of me?"

"That, perhaps, you had better not inquire."

"I prefer to know the worst."

"She said you encouraged the attentions of her nephew, forgetting the difference in social position, and also that your connections were not of a sort to recommend you. I admit, Miss Linden, that you are very ladylike in appearance, but, I can hardly be expected to admit into my house, in the important position of governess to my child, the daughter or niece of an apple-woman."

"Did Mrs. Leighton say that I was related to an

apple-woman?"

"Yes, Miss Linden. I own I was surprised."

"It is not true, Mrs. Cole."

"You live in the house of such a person, do you not?"

"Yes, she is an humble friend of mine, and has been kind to me."

"You cannot be very fastidious. However, that is your own affair. I am sorry to disappoint you, Miss Linden, but it will be quite impossible for me to employ you."

"Then I will bid you good-morning, Mrs. Cole," said Florence, sore at heart.

"Good-morning. You will, I think, understand my position. If you applied for a position in one of the public schools, I don't think that your residence would be an objection."

Florence left the house, sad and despondent. She saw that Mrs. Leighton, by her unfriendly representations, would prevent her from getting any opportunity to teach. She must seek some more humble employment.

"Well, Florence, did you get a place?" asked Mrs. O'Keefe, as she passed that lady's stand.

"No, Mrs. O'Keefe," answered Florence, wearily.

"And why not? Did the woman think you didn't know enough?"

"She objected to me because I was not living in a fashionable quarter - at least that was one of her objections."

"I'm sure you've got a nate, clane home, and it looks as nate as wax all the time."

"It isn't exactly stylish," said Florence, with a faint smile.

"You are, at any rate. What does the woman want, I'd like to know?"

"She doesn't want me. It seems Mrs. Leighton did not speak very highly of me."

"The trollop! I'd like to give her a box on the ear, drat her impudence!" said the irate apple-woman. "And what will you be doin' now?"

"Do you think I can get some sewing to do, Mrs. O'Keefe?"

"Yes, Miss Florence - I'll get you some vests to make; but it's hard work and poor pay."

"I must take what I can get," sighed Florence. "I cannot choose."

"If you'd only tend an apple-stand, Miss Florence! There's Mrs. Brady wants to sell out on account of the rheumatics, and I've got a trifle in the savings bank - enough to buy it. You'd make a dollar a day, easy."

"It isn't to be thought of, Mrs. O'Keefe. If you will kindly see about getting me some sewing, I will see how I can get along."

The result was that Mrs. O'Keefe brought Florence in the course of the day half a dozen vests, for which she was to be paid the munificent sum of twenty-five cents each.

Florence had very little idea of what she was undertaking.

She was an expert needlewoman, and proved adequate to the work, but with her utmust industry she could only make one vest in a day, and that would barely pay her rent.

True, she had some money laid aside on which she could draw, but that would soon be expended, and then what was to become of her?

"Shure, I won't let you starve, Florence," said the warm-hearted apple-woman.

"But, Mrs. O'Keefe, I can't consent to live on you."

"And why not? I'm well and strong, and I'm makin' more money than I nade."

"I couldn't think of it, though I thank you for your kindness."

"Shure, you might write a letter to your uncle, Florence."

"He would expect me, in that case, to consent to a marriage with Curtis. You wouldn't advise me to do that?"

"No; he's a mane blackguard, and I'd say it to his face."

Weeks rolled by, and Florence began to show the effects of hard work and confinement.

She grew pale and thin, and her face was habitually sad.

She had husbanded her savings as a governess as closely as she could, but in spite of all her economy it dwindled till she had none left.

Henceforth, she must depend on twenty-five cents a day, and this seemed well-nigh impossible.

In this emergency the pawnbroker occurred to her.

She had a variety of nice dresses, and she had also a handsome ring, given her by her uncle on her last birthday.

This she felt sure must have cost fifty dollars.

It was a trial to part with it, but there seemed to be no alternative.

"If my uncle has withdrawn his affection from me," she said to herself, "why should I scruple to pawn the ring? It is the symbol of a love that no longer exists."

So she entered the pawnbrowker's - the first that attracted her attention - and held out the ring.

"How much will you lend me on this?" she asked, half frightened at finding herself in such a place.

The pawnbroker examined it carefully. His practiced eye at once detected its value, but it was not professional to admit this.

"Rings is a drug in the market, young lady," he said. "I've got more than I know what to do with. I'll give you four - four dollars."

"Four dollars!" repeated Florence, in dismay. "Why, it must have cost fifty. It was bought in Tiffany's."

"You are mistaken, my dear. Did you buy it yourself there?"

"No, my uncle gave it to me."

"He may have said he paid fifty dollars for it," said the pawnbroker, wagging his head, "but we know better."

"But what will you give?" asked Florence, desperately.

"I'll give you five dollars, and not a penny more," said the broker, surveying her distressed face, shrewdly. "You can take it or not."

What could Florence do?

She must have money, and feared that no other pawnbroker would give her more.

"Make out the ticket, then," she said, wearily, with a sigh.

This was done, and she left the place, half timid, half ashamed, and wholly discouraged.

But the darkest hour is sometimes nearest the dawn. A great overwhelming surprise awaited her. She had scarcely left the shop when a glad voice cried:

"I have found you at last, Florence!"

She looked up and saw - Dodger.

But not the old Dodger. She saw a nicely dressed young gentleman, larger than the friend she had parted with six months before, with a brighter, more intelligent, and manly look.

"Dodger!" she faltered.

"Yes, it is Dodger."

"Where did you come from?"

"From San Francisco. But what have you been doing there?"

And Dodger pointed in the direction of the pawn-broker's shop.

"I pawned my ring."

"Then I shall get it back at once. How much did you get on it?"

"Five dollars."

"Give me the ticket, and go in with me."

The pawnbroker was very reluctant to part with the ring, which he made sure would not be reclaimed; but there was no help for it.

As they emerged into the street, Dodger said: "I've come back to restore you to your rights, and give Curtis Waring the most disagreeable surprise he ever had. Come home, and I'll tell you all about it. I've struck luck, Florence, and you're going to share it."

CHAPTER XXXVI

MRS. O'KEEFE IN A NEW ROLE

No time was lost in seeing Bolton and arranging a plan of campaign.

Curtis Waring, nearing the accomplishment of his plans, was far from anticipating impending disaster.

His uncle's health had become so poor, and his strength had been so far undermined, that it was thought desirable to employ a sick nurse. An advertisement was inserted in a morning paper, which luckily attracted the attention of Bolton.

"You must go, Mrs. O'Keefe," he said to the applewoman. "It is important that we have some one in the house - some friend of Florence and the boy - to watch what is going on."

"Bridget O'Keefe is no fool. Leave her to manage."

The result was that among a large number of applicants Mrs. O'Keefe was selected by Curtis as Mr. Linden's nurse, as she expressed herself willing to work for four dollars a week, while the lowest outside demand was seven.

We will now enter the house, in which the last scenes of our story are to take place.

Mr. Linden, weak and emaciated, was sitting in an easy-chair in his library.

"How do you feel this morning, uncle?" asked Curtis, entering the room.

"I am very weak, Curtis. I don't think I shall ever be any better."

"I have engaged a nurse, uncle, as you desired, and I expect her this morning."

"That is well, Curtis. I do not wish to confine you to my bedside."

"The nurse is below," said Jane, the servant, entering.

"Send her up."

Mrs. O'Keefe entered in the sober attire of a nurse. She dropped a curtsey.

"Are you the nurse I engaged?" said Curtis.

"Yes, sir."

"Your name, please."

"Mrs. Barnes, sir."

"Have you experience as a nurse?"

"Plenty, sir."

"Uncle, this is Mrs. Barnes, your new nurse. I hope you will find her satisfactory."

"She looks like a good woman," said Mr. Linden, feebly. "I think she will suit me."

"Indade, sir, I'll try."

"Uncle," said Curtis, "I have to go downtown. I have some business to attend to. I leave you in the care of Mrs. Barnes."

"Shure, I'll take care of him, sir."

"Is there anything I can do for you, Mr. Linden?" asked the new nurse, in a tone of sympathy.

"Can you minister to a mind diseased?"

"I'll take the best care of you, Mr. Linden, but it isn't as if you had a wife or daughter."

"Ah, that is a sore thought! I have no wife or daughter; but I have a niece."

"And where is she, sir?"

"I don't know. I drove her from me by my unkindness. I repent bitterly, but it's now too late."

"And why don't you send for her to come home?"

"I would gladly do so, but I don't know where she is. Curtis has tried to find her, but in vain. He says she is in Chicago."

"And what should take her to Chicago?"

"He says she is there as a governess in a family."

"By the brow of St. Patrick!" thought Mrs. O'Keefe, "if that Curtis isn't a natural-born liar. I'm sure she'd come back if you'd send for her, sir," said she, aloud.

"Do you think so?" asked Linden, eagerly.

"I'm sure of it."

"But I don't know where to send."

"I know of a party that would be sure to find her."

"Who is it?"

"It's a young man. They call him Dodger. If any one can find Miss Florence, he can."

"You know my niece's name?"

"I have heard it somewhere. From Mr. Waring, I think."

"And you think this young man would agree to go to Chicago and find her?"

"Yes, sir, I make bold to say he will."

"Tell him to go at once. He will need money. In yonder desk you will find a picture of my niece and a roll of bills. Give them to him and send him at once."

"Yes, sir, I will. But if you'll take my advice, you won't

say anything to Mr. Curtis. He might think it foolish."

"True! If your friend succeeds, we'll give Curtis a surprise."

"And a mighty disagreeable one, I'll be bound," soliloquized Mrs. O'Keefe.

"I think, Mrs. Barnes, I will retire to my chamber, if you will assist me."

She assisted Mr. Linden to his room, and then returned to the library.

"Mrs. Barnes, there's a young man inquiring for you," said Jane, entering.

"Send him in, Jane."

The visitor was Dodger, neatly dressed.

"How are things going, Mrs. O'Keefe?" he asked.

"Splendid, Dodger. Here's some money for you."

"What for?"

"You're to go to Chicago and bring back Florence."

"But she isn't there."

"Nivir mind. You're to pretend to go."

"But that won't take money."

"Give it to Florence, then. It's hers by rights. Won't we

give Curtis a surprise? Where's his wife?"

"I have found a comfortable boarding house for her. When had we better carry out this programme? She's very anxious to see her husband."

"The more fool she. Kape her at home and out of his sight, or there's no knowin' what he'll do. And, Dodger, dear, kape an eye on the apple-stand. I mistrust Mrs. Burke that's runnin' it."

"I will. Does the old gentleman seem to be very sick?"

"He's wake as a rat. Curtis would kill him soon if we didn't interfere. But we'll soon circumvent him, the snake in the grass! Miss Florence will soon come to her own, and Curtis Waring will be out in the cold."

"The most I have against him is that he tried to marry Florence when he had a wife already."

"He's as bad as they make 'em, Dodger. It won't be my fault if Mr. Linden's eyes are not opened to his wickedness."

CHAPTER XXXVII

THE DIPLOMACY OF MRS. O'KEEFE

Mrs. O'Keefe was a warm-hearted woman, and the sad, drawn face of Mr. Linden appealed to her pity.

"Why should I let the poor man suffer when I can relieve him?" she asked herself.

So the next morning, after Curtis had, according to his custom, gone downtown, being in the invalid's sick chamber, she began to act in a mysterious manner. She tiptoed to the door, closed it and approached Mr. Linden's bedside with the air of one about to unfold a strange story.

"Whist now," she said, with her finger on her lips.

"What is the matter?" asked the invalid, rather alarmed.

"Can you bear a surprise, sir?"

"Have you any bad news for me?"

"No; it's good news, but you must promise not to tell Curtis."

"Is it about Florence? Your messenger can hardly have

reached Chicago."

"He isn't going there, sir."

"But you promised that he should," said Mr. Linden, disturbed.

"I'll tell you why, sir. Florence is not in Chicago."

"I - I don't understand. You said she was there."

"Begging your pardon, sir, it was Curtis that said so, though he knew she was in New York."

"But what motive could he have had for thus misrepresenting matters?"

"He doesn't want you to take her back."

"I can't believe you, Mrs. Barnes. He loves her, and wants to marry her."

"He couldn't marry her if she consented to take him."

"Why not? Mrs. Barnes, you confuse me."

"I won't deceive you as he has done. There's rason in plinty. He's married already."

"Is this true?" demanded Mr. Linden, in excitement.

"It's true enough; more by token, to-morrow, whin he's out, his wife will come here and tell you so herself."

"But who are you who seem to know so much about my family?"

"I'm a friend of the pore girl you've driven from the house, because she would not marry a rascally spalpeen that's been schemin' to get your property into his hands."

"You're a friend of Florence? Where is she?"

"She's in my house, and has been there ever since she left her home."

"Is she - well?"

"As well as she can be whin she's been workin' her fingers to the bone wid sewin' to keep from starvin'."

"My God! what have I done?"

"You've let Curtis Waring wind you around his little finger - that's what you've done, Mr. Linden."

"How soon can I see Florence?"

"How soon can you bear it?"

"The sooner the better."

"Then it'll be to-morrow, I'm thinkin', that is if you won't tell Curtis."

"No, no; I promise."

"I'll manage everything, sir. Don't worry now."

Mr. Linden's face lost its anxious look - so that when, later in the day, Curtis looked into the room he was surprised.

"My uncle looks better," he said.

"Yes, sir," answered the nurse. "I've soothed him like."

"Indeed! You seem to be a very accomplished nurse."

"Faith, that I am, sir, though it isn't I that should say it."

"May I ask how you soothed him?" inquired Curtis, anxiously.

"I told him that Miss Florence would soon be home."

"I do not think it right to hold out hopes that may prove ill-founded."

"I know what I am about, Mr. Curtis."

"I dare say you understand your business, Mrs. Barnes, but if my uncle should be disappointed, I am afraid the consequences will be lamentable."

"Do you think he'll live long, sir?"

Curtis shrugged his shoulders.

"It is very hard to tell. My uncle is a very feeble man."

"And if he dies, I suppose the property goes to you?"

"I suppose so."

"But where does Florence come in?"

"It seems to me, Mrs. Barnes, that you take a good deal

of interest in our family affairs," said Curtis, suspiciously.

"That's true, sir. Why shouldn't I take an interest in a nice gentleman like you?"

Curtis smiled.

"I am doing my best to find Florence. Then our marriage will take place, and it matters little to whom the property is left."

"But I thought Miss Florence didn't care to marry you?"

"It is only because she thinks cousins ought not to marry. It's a foolish fancy, and she'll get over it."

"Thrue for you, sir. My first husband was my cousin, and we always agreed, barrin' an occasional fight -"

"I don't think Florence and I will ever fight, Mrs. Barnes."

"What surprises me, Mr. Curtis, is that a nice-lookin' gentleman like you hasn't been married before."

Curtis eyed her keenly, but her face told him nothing.

"I never saw one I wanted to marry till my cousin grew up," he said.

"I belave in marryin', meself. I was first married at sivinteen."

"How long ago was that, Mrs. Barnes?"

"It's long ago, Mr. Curtis. I'm an old woman now. I was thirty-five last birthday."

Curtis came near laughing outright, for he suspected - what was true - that the nurse would never see her fiftieth birthday again.

"Then you are just my age," he said.

"If I make him laugh he won't suspect nothing," soliloquized the wily nurse. "That's a pretty big lie, even for me."

"Shure I look older, Mr. Curtis," she said, aloud. "What wid the worry of losin' two fond husbands, I look much older than you."

"Oh, your are very well preserved, Mrs. Barnes."

Curtis went into his uncle's chamber.

"How are you feeling, uncle?" he asked.

"I think I am better," answered Mr. Linden, coldly, for he had not forgotten Mrs. Barnes' revelations.

"That is right. Only make an effort, and you will soon be strong again."

"I think I may. I may live ten years to annoy you."

"I fervently hope so," said Curtis, but there was a false ring in his voice that his uncle detected. "How do you like the new nurse?"

"She is helping me wonderfully. You made a

good selection."

"I will see that she is soon discharged," Curtis inwardly resolved. "If her being here is to prolong my uncle's life, and keep me still waiting for the estate, I must clear the house of her."

"You must not allow her to buoy you up with unfounded hopes. She has been telling you that Florence will soon return."

"Yes; she seems convinced of it."

"Of course she knows nothing of it. She may return, but I doubt whether she is in Chicago now. I think the family she was with has gone to Europe."

"Where did you hear that, Curtis?" asked Mr. Linden, with unwonted sharpness.

"I have sources of information which at present I do not care to impart. Rest assured that I am doing all I can to get her back."

"You still want to marry her, Curtis?"

"I do, most certainly."

"I shall not insist upon it. I should not have done so before."

"Have you changed your mind, uncle?"

"Yes; I have made a mistake, and I have decided to correct it."

"What has come over him?" Curtis asked himself. "Some influence hostile to me has been brought to bear. It must be that nurse. I will quietly dismiss her to-morrow, paying her a week's wages, in lieu of warning. She's evidently a meddler."

CHAPTER XXXVIII

THE CLOSING SCENE

The next day Tim Bolton, dressed in a jaunty style, walked up the steps of the Linden mansion.

"Is Mr. Waring at home?" he asked.

"No, sir; he has gone downtown."

"I'll step in and wait for him. Please show me to the library."

Jane, who had been taken into confidence by the nurse, showed him at once into the room mentioned.

Half an hour later Curtis entered.

"How long have you been here, Bolton?"

"But a short time. You sent for me?"

"I did."

"On business?"

"Well, yes."

"Is there anything new?"

"Yes, my uncle is failing fast."

"Is he likely to die soon?"

"I shouldn't be surprised if he died within a week."

"I suspect Curtis means to help him! Well, what has that to do with me?" he asked. "You will step into the property, of course?"

"There is a little difficulty in the way which I can overcome with your help."

"What is it?"

"I can't get him to give up the foolish notion that the boy he lost is still alive."

"It happens to be true."

"Yes; but he must not know it. Before he dies I want him to make a new will, revoking all others, leaving all the property to me."

"Will he do it?"

"I don't know. As long as he thinks the boy is living, I don't believe he will. You see what a drawback that is."

"I see. What can I do to improve the situation?"

"I want you to sign a paper confessing that you abducted the boy -"

"At your instigation?"

"That must not be mentioned. You will go on to say that a year or two later - the time is not material - he died of typhoid fever. You can say that you did not dare to reveal this before, but do so now, impelled by remorse."

"Have you got it written out? I can't remember all them words."

"Yes; here it is."

"All right," said Bolton, taking the paper and tucking it into an inside pocket. "I'll copy it out in my own handwriting. How much are you going to give me for doing this?"

"A thousand dollars."

"Cash?"

"I can't do that. I have met with losses at the gaming table, and I don't dare ask money from my uncle at this time. He thinks I am thoroughly steady."

"At how much do you value the estate?"

"At four hundred thousand dollars. I wormed it out of my uncle's lawyer the other day."

"And you expect me to help you to that amount for only a thousand dollars?"

"A thousand dollars is a good deal of money."

"And so is four hundred thousand. After all, your uncle may not die."

"He is sure to."

"You seem very confident."

"And with good reason. Leave that to me. I promise you, on my honor, to pay you two thousand dollars when I get the estate."

"But what is going to happen to poor Dodger, the rightful heir?"

"Well, let it be three hundred dollars a year, then."

"Where is he now?"

"I don't mind telling you, as it can do no harm. He is in California."

"Whew! That was smart. How did you get him there?"

"I drugged him, and had him sent on board a ship bound for San Francisco, around Cape Horn. The fact is, I was getting a little suspicious of you, and I wanted to put you beyond the reach of temptation."

"You are a clever rascal, Curtis. After all, suppose the prize should slip through your fingers?"

"It won't. I have taken every precaution."

"When do you want this document?"

"Bring it back to me this afternoon, copied and signed.

That is all you have to do; I will attend to the rest."

While this conversation was going on there were unseen listeners.

Behind a portiere Mrs. Barnes, the nurse, and John Linden heard every word that was said.

"And what do you think now, sir?" whispered Mrs. O'Keefe (to give her real name).

"It is terrible. I would not have believed Curtis capable of such a crime. But is it really true, Mrs. Barnes? Is my lost boy alive?"

"To be sure he is."

"Have you seen him?"

"I know him as well as I know you, sir, and better, too."

"Is he - tell me, is he a good boy? Curtis told me that he might be a criminal."

"He might, but he isn't. He's as dacent and honest a boy as iver trod shoe leather. You'll be proud of him, sir."

"But he's in California."

"He was; but he's got back. You shall see him to-day, and Florence, too. Hark! I hear the door bell. They're here now. I think you had better go in and confront Curtis."

"I feel weak, Mrs. Barnes. Let me lean on you."

"You can do that, and welcome, sir."

The nurse pushed aside the portiere, and the two entered the library - Mrs. Barnes rotund and smiling, Mr. Linden gaunt and spectral looking, like one risen from the grave.

Curtis eyed the pair with a startled look.

"Mrs. Barnes," he said, angrily, "what do you mean by taking my uncle from his bed and bringing him down here? It is as much as his life is worth. You seem unfit for your duties as nurse. You will leave the house tomorrow, and I will engage a substitute."

"I shall lave whin I git ready, Mr. Curtis Waring," said the nurse, her arms akimbo. "Maybe somebody else will lave the house. Me and Mr. Linden have been behind the curtain for twenty minutes, and he has heard every word you said."

Curtis turned livid, and his heart sank.

"It's true, Curtis," said John Linden's hollow voice. "I have heard all. It was you who abducted my boy, and have made my life a lonely one all these years. Oh, man! man! how could you have the heart to do it?"

Curtis stared at him with parched lips, unable to speak.

"Not content with this, you drove from the house my dear niece, Florence. You made me act cruelly toward her. I fear she will not forgive me."

But just then the door opened, and Florence, rushing into the room, sank at her uncle's feet.

"Oh, uncle," she said, "will you take me back?"

"Yes, Florence, never again to leave me. And who is this?" he asked, fixing his eyes on Dodger, who stood shyly in the doorway.

"I'll tell you, sir," said Tim Bolton. "That is your own son, whom I stole away from you when he was a kid, being hired to do it by Curtis Waring."

"It's a lie," said Curtis, hoarsely.

"Come to me, my boy," said Mr. Linden, with a glad light in his eyes.

"At last Heaven has heard my prayers," he ejaculated. "We will never be separated. I was ready to die, but now I hope to live for many years. I feel that I have a new lease of life."

With a baffled growl Curtis Waring darted a furious look at the three.

"That boy is an impostor," he said. "They are deceiving you."

"He is my son. I see his mother's look in his face. As for you, Curtis Waring, my eyes are open at last to your villainy. You deserve nothing at my hands; but I will make some provision for you."

There was another surprise.

Curtis Waring's deserted wife, brought from California by Dodger, entered the room, leading by the hand a young child.

"Oh, Curtis," she said, reproachfully. "How could you leave me? I have come to you, my husband, with our little child."

"Begone! woman!" said Curtis, furiously. "I will never receive or recognize you!"

"Oh, sir!" she said, turning to Mr. Linden, "what shall I do?"

"Curtis Waring," said Mr. Linden, sternly, "unless you receive this woman and treat her properly, you shall receive nothing from me."

"And if I do?"

"You will receive an income of two thousand dollars a year, payable quarterly. Mrs. Waring, you will remain here with your child till your husband provides another home for you."

Curtis slunk out of the room, but he was too wise to refuse his uncle's offer.

He and his wife are living in Chicago, and he treats her fairly well, fearing that, otherwise, he will lose his income.

Mr. Linden looks ten years younger than he did at the opening of the story.

Florence and Dodger - now known as Harvey Linden - live with him.

Dodger, under a competent private tutor, is making up the deficiencies in his education.

It is early yet to speak of marriage, but it is possible that Florence may marry a cousin, after all.

Tim Bolton has turned over a new leaf, given up his saloon, and is carrying on a country hotel within fifty miles of New York.

He has five thousand dollars in the bank, presented by Dodger, with his father's sanction, and is considered quite a reputable citizen.

As for Mrs. O'Keefe, she still keeps the apple-stand, being unwilling to give it up; but she, too, has a handsome sum in the bank, and calls often upon her two children, as she calls them.

In the midst of their prosperity Florence and Dodger will never forget the time when they were adrift in New York.

George Eliot
George Gissing
George MacDonald
George Meredith
George Orwell
George Sylvester Viereck
George Tucker
George W. Cable
George Wharton James
Gertrude Atherton
Gordon Casserly
Grace E. King
Grace Gallatin
Grace Greenwood
Grant Allen
Guillermo A. Sherwell
Gulielma Zollinger
Gustav Flaubert
H. A. Cody
H. B. Irving
H.C. Bailey
H. G. Wells
H. H. Munro
H. Irving Hancock
H. Rider Haggard
H. W. C. Davis
Haldeman Julius
Hall Caine
Hamilton Wright Mabie
Hans Christian Andersen
Harold Avery
Harold McGrath
Harriet Beecher Stowe
Harry Castlemon
Harry Coghill
Harry Houidini
Hayden Carruth
Helent Hunt Jackson
Helen Nicolay
Hendrik Conscience
Hendy David Thoreau
Henri Barbusse
Henrik Ibsen
Henry Adams
Henry Ford
Henry Frost
Henry James
Henry Jones Ford
Henry Seton Merriman
Henry W Longfellow
Herbert A. Giles
Herbert Carter
Herbert N. Casson
Herman Hesse
Hildegard G. Frey
Homer
Honore De Balzac
Horace B. Day
Horace Walpole
Horatio Alger Jr.
Howard Pyle
Howard R. Garis
Hugh Lofting
Hugh Walpole
Humphry Ward
Ian Maclaren
Inez Haynes Gillmore
Irving Bacheller
Isabel Hornibrook
Israel Abrahams
Ivan Turgenev
J.G.Austin
J. Henri Fabre
J. M. Barrie
J. Macdonald Oxley
J. S. Fletcher
J. S. Knowles
J. Storer Clouston
Jack London
Jacob Abbott
James Allen
James Andrews
James Baldwin
James Branch Cabell
James DeMille
James Joyce
James Lane Allen
James Lane Allen
James Oliver Curwood
James Oppenheim
James Otis
James R. Driscoll
Jane Austen
Jane L. Stewart
Janet Aldridge
Jens Peter Jacobsen
Jerome K. Jerome
John Burroughs
John Cournos
John F. Kennedy
John Gay
John Glasworthy
John Habberton
John Joy Bell
John Kendrick Bangs
John Milton
John Philip Sousa
Jonas Lauritz Idemil Lie
Jonathan Swift
Joseph A. Altsheler
Joseph Carey
Joseph Conrad
Joseph E. Badger Jr
Joseph Hergesheimer
Joseph Jacobs
Jules Vernes
Julian Hawthrone
Julie A Lippmann
Justin Huntly McCarthy
Kakuzo Okakura
Kenneth Grahame
Kenneth McGaffey
Kate Langley Bosher
Kate Langley Bosher
Katherine Cecil Thurston
Katherine Stokes
L. A. Abbot
L. T. Meade
L. Frank Baum
Latta Griswold
Laura Dent Crane
Laura Lee Hope
Laurence Housman
Lawrence Beasley
Leo Tolstoy
Leonid Andreyev
Lewis Carroll
Lewis Sperry Chafer
Lilian Bell
Lloyd Osbourne
Louis Hughes
Louis Tracy
Louisa May Alcott
Lucy Fitch Perkins
Lucy Maud Montgomery
Luther Benson
Lydia Miller Middleton
Lyndon Orr
M. Corvus
M. H. Adams
Margaret E. Sangster
Margret Howth
Margaret Vandercook

Margret Penrose
Maria Edgeworth
Maria Thompson Daviess
Mariano Azuela
Marion Polk Angellotti
Mark Overton
Mark Twain
Mary Austin
Mary Catherine Crowley
Mary Cole
Mary Hastings Bradley
Mary Roberts Rinehart
Mary Rowlandson
M. Wollstonecraft Shelley
Maud Lindsay
Max Beerbohm
Myra Kelly
Nathaniel Hawthrone
Nicolo Machiavelli
O. F. Walton
Oscar Wilde
Owen Johnson
P.G. Wodehouse
Paul and Mabel Thorne
Paul G. Tomlinson
Paul Severing
Percy Brebner
Peter B. Kyne
Plato
R. Derby Holmes
R. L. Stevenson
R. S. Ball
Rabindranath Tagore
Rahul Alvares
Ralph Bonehill
Ralph Henry Barbour
Ralph Victor
Ralph Waldo Emmerson
Rene Descartes
Rex Beach
Rex E. Beach
Richard Harding Davis
Richard Jefferies
Richard Le Gallienne
Robert Barr
Robert Frost
Robert Gordon Anderson
Robert L. Drake
Robert Lansing
Robert Lynd
Robert Michael Ballantyne
Robert W. Chambers
Rosa Nouchette Carey
Rudyard Kipling
Samuel B. Allison
Samuel Hopkins Adams
Sarah Bernhardt
Sarah C. Hallowell
Selma Lagerlof
Sherwood Anderson
Sigmund Freud
Standish O'Grady
Stanley Weyman
Stella Benson
Stella M. Francis
Stephen Crane
Stewart Edward White
Stijn Streuvels
Swami Abhedananda
Swami Parmananda
T. S. Ackland
T. S. Arthur
The Princess Der Ling
Thomas A. Janvier
Thomas A Kempis
Thomas Anderton
Thomas Bailey Aldrich
Thomas Bulfinch
Thomas De Quincey
Thomas Dixon
Thomas H. Huxley
Thomas Hardy
Thomas More
Thornton W. Burgess
U. S. Grant
Valentine Williams
Various Authors
Vaughan Kester
Victor Appleton
Victoria Cross
Virginia Woolf
Wadsworth Camp
Walter Camp
Walter Scott
Washington Irving
Wilbur Lawton
Wilkie Collins
Willa Cather
Willard F. Baker
William Dean Howells
William le Queux
W. Makepeace Thackeray
William W. Walter
William Shakespeare
Winston Churchill
Yei Theodora Ozaki
Yogi Ramacharaka
Young E. Allison
Zane Grey

www.ingramcontent.com/pod-product-compliance
Lightning Source LLC
LaVergne TN
LVHW091639100826
845152LV00006B/101/J

* 9 7 8 1 4 2 1 8 2 3 8 7 4 *